WILD OATS

On Avenal's Kettleman Plain

Text and Illustrations by
Perry Leon Huffman

Note for Librarians: A cataloguing record for this book is available from Library and Archives Canada at www.collectionscanada.ca/amicus/index-e.html
ISBN 1-4120-5891-0

Printed in Victoria, BC, Canada. Printed on paper with minimum 30% recycled fibre. Trafford's print shop runs on "green energy" from solar, wind and other environmentally-friendly power sources.

TRAFFORD
PUBLISHING

Offices in Canada, USA, Ireland and UK

This book was published on-demand in cooperation with Trafford Publishing. On-demand publishing is a unique process and service of making a book available for retail sale to the public taking advantage of on-demand manufacturing and Internet marketing. On-demand publishing includes promotions, retail sales, manufacturing, order fulfilment, accounting and collecting royalties on behalf of the author.

Book sales for North America and international:
Trafford Publishing, 6E–2333 Government St.,
Victoria, BC v8t 4p4 CANADA
phone 250 383 6864 (toll-free 1 888 232 4444)
fax 250 383 6804; email to orders@trafford.com
Book sales in Europe:
Trafford Publishing (UK) Limited, 9 Park End Street, 2nd Floor
Oxford, UK ox1 1hh UNITED KINGDOM
phone 44 (0)1865 722 113 (local rate 0845 230 9601)
facsimile 44 (0)1865 722 868; info.uk@trafford.com

10 9 8 7 6 5 4 3 2

Avenal

(Avena is Spanish meaning oats
or… field of oats)

INTRODUCTION

I WAS pretty small when I first became aware that Avenal was a very special place, that everybody liked it and they all wanted to live there.

As I went through the grades in school, the town and I evolved into what we had become. I came to Avenal as a two-year-old boy and left as a seventeen year-old high school graduate. There was no work for me and the oil field was closing down. And I was gone with the oil and lots of good paying jobs.

And...finally, the rusty oil derricks are gone along with the fields of wild oats.

The townspeople now have come full circle. Pop and many of his friends were farm labors at times, before they came to Avenal to work the fields of oil. The houses continue to shelter field workers, but ones arriving too late for harvesting oil.

The valley is a growing and changing place that is responding to pressures of economic survival. The large and small valley towns are struggling to meet new needs and are changing before our eyes. Form does follow function.

I have become one of those occasional "Avenal tourists" the locals find curious and a little annoying. We are those old folks who drive slowly around town, holding up traffic while gawking at the astounding changes...sidewalks and gutters?

Who knows what closing the ancient alkaline sagebrush land to agriculture... just over the Kettleman Hills will bring to Avenal, as time rolls on and sagebrush again reclaims parts of the old alkali flats?

My writer friend of many years, Eddie Lopez, read my

personal family stories and thought I ought to rewrite them into a book with more of Avenal's history.

Eddie sent the stories to respected California author, Gerald Haslem to look over. Haslem said there needed to be some historical information and some rewriting to make it more of an Avenal book of some historical interest.

You have in your hands a personal time capsule of my small place in the history of a very special valley town, told in my voice and in the age and attitude of those distant times. These are glimpses of some of my boyhood experiences, during the brightest bloom in a young Avenal.

Brothers, Basil and Jesse spent most of each day, week and year experiencing their own Avenal. Each of us was impressed in some different adventures.

The history timeline…you will find in the ending notes… enjoy.

Thank you

The good people of Avenal, my parents, my family
and my good friends, all came together to help make
this book a reality. Wild Oats is dedicated to them
and those of you who follow us.

TABLE OF CONTENTS

Me and Lloyd and my new house. Dad built it.

the Big Ditch ↓

1. 1943 - THE BEST TOWN AROUND

THE NEW kid in the neighborhood is about my age because he says he is going to be in the third grade. His name is Lloyd, he has piercing pale blue eyes, dark tanned skin, real white blond hair and comes from Oklahoma.

He moved out here with his family all the way across the country…through all those towns and states…and can you believe they picked out Avenal as the best place a guy could live in? Almost all the kids in town are from far away places like Oklahoma, Tennessee, Arkansas, Missouri, Texas and just…everywhere.

I guess Avenal has to be a really good place. People know about it all over the country and travel hundreds and thousands of miles to live here. People seem to figure it is about the best town around.

I am pretty lucky to be living in just the right place any-one could be. And we have a brand new home with a cool cemented basement that my Dad built in just about two years…all by himself, on his time off from working in the oil fields. He went to the library to read about the plumbing, electricity and stuff.

Sometimes, me and my brother Basil, walk about a mile across town to the library and read or check out free books. It is a good deal.

Our schools are almost new and our picture show is fancy and it's almost new. The high school swimming pool we play in during the summer is very nice with tile trim and it's really a good place to be when it's hot. I go off the high board and can swim under water across the pool and part way back. Sometimes I like to pretend that I am Aquaman.

Everything that wasn't moved up from Taft, Coalinga or other places by oil companies isn't very old. And our house is the newest and best house in the whole town. I guess I am about the luckiest guy my age that I know, around here. Life is good for me.

My Dad is real smart and is the best at everything he does and Mom can cook stuff that hardly anybody ever heard of in Avenal. Her dad has been a cook on ocean liners out of San Francisco to the Hawaiian Islands. He knows some fancy cooking and my Mom learned a lot from him.

We are eating fine and having some good times while our fighting men are beating the hell out of the Germans and Japs who are trying to take over the world. Hitler and Tojo both think they have the best country and want to kill every one else.

We see it all on the Saturday newsreels at the show along with two feature movies, a cartoon and a serial special. They ought to just kill each other and leave America alone. We have everybody here from different countries getting along pretty good, including people from Germany and Japan.

Nobody has a chance against America. We are the newest, best and bravest place in the whole world. We even have the Marines and guys like John Wayne. No one is going to beat us.

We help Dad with the blackout drills in town and air patrol watches. We watch for Jap planes from the fire lookout station in the hills south west of town. We still haven't caught any airplanes flying in to bomb us.

If I ever catch any of those sons of bitches, I'm ready to give them a real good cuss'n. I have been paying attention and practicing...when there are no girls or grownups around to hear.

My older brother, Basil Jr. goes with us on the air patrol watch but younger brother Jesse is too little to go. Basil teases and pesters me to no end but Jesse is about four years younger than me and is too small to tease or be any real bother.

The oil fields are important in the war and have to be guarded against spies who want to sneak in and blow the whole place up.

With the war going on, meat and about every thing else is rationed. There are ration stamps for everything and you just get your share of stamps to buy stuff.

Dad built chicken pens and coops and rabbit hutches so we eat our own eggs, fried chicken and fried rabbit. We get to save all the meat stamps just for hamburger and steak.

We even have a garden...but it just does pretty good, with chard, onions, radishes and peppers. Mom cans the peppers and they are hot. But we eat them to show how tough we are and that we aren't scared of anything. Sometimes, Dad will buy some olives and cure them in a big crock then we put them up in jars. They are the best.

We are luckier than most of the kids in our neighborhood who don't have a new house or all the neat things my Dad figures out for us. Like the vacations he plans out of Avenal, west to the ocean, east to the mountains and north to San Francisco and Navato. My Grandpa and Grandma Hiribarren's house is up north.

When Grandpa Huffman retired, he moved to Avenal from Winsor and lives about three houses over toward downtown. Basil and I take turns visiting, hearing stories and sleeping there on Friday or Saturday nights. I was named after Grandpa Perry Huffman and Basil was named after Dad who was named after his Uncle Basil Cessna. My middle name is Leon after great grandpa Captain Leon Hiribarren who was French Basque, sailed the seas, San Francisco Bay and became a San Francisco Bay Area businessman. Little brother Jesse Orval was named after Uncle Orval Allen, Dad's sister's husband. Uncle Orvil is really a good guy.

Some of our neighbors and friends here in Avenal are real interesting people who are funny and kind of strange. That's probably why we have some odd things happening around here. It never gets slow for very long at our place.

I like to listen to the funny stories everybody tells when we have company drop by. There is usually something to drink and often a visit will take more than one trip to Rice's liquor store.

Some of the same family stories are told to different people more than once and those are the ones I remember and are the best.

There are people who don't have nice homes and family and they go to bars to visit. I've heard people say there are about the same number of churches as there are bars...with the good fighting the bad and coming out just about Even-Steven.

They say for a while, after the big oil strike, there were two or three whorehouses in Avenal. Places where rough-necks, roustabouts, drillers, tool pushers and most everyone else sowed their wild oats.

Families and churches came in and ran them all off. They are real bad places to have in a good town like ours.

I was born in Coalinga, which is about seventeen miles north of Avenal, but we moved right on down here when I was about two and we just stayed put...not counting travel-ing on vacations.

Most of the kids in my class started kindergarten with me but we do get a new kid, like Lloyd, or have one move away and then sometimes they'd move right back again. Avenal is hard to beat.

2. THE GREAT AVENAL
TRAIN ROBBERY

MOVIES will put some wild ideas in your head. Like the plan we cooked up to rob the Avenal train.

Saturday is a special day for us on the Kettleman Plain below the oil fields down here in Avenal. Our folks give us each eleven cents for our ticket to the Saturday matinee, which has double features, a newsreel, a cartoon and a weekly adventure serial that you don't ever want to miss.

We live near the east edge of town and the picture show is near the west edge of town and the walk is just under a mile and might take fifteen minutes, more or less, depending on our excitement.

In the summer time, we go barefoot and always have a time getting around the puncture vines on the way to the show. The dirt doesn't get too hot but the blacktop streets soak up the sun 'til it'll blister you feet. You have to make a run for it to get around the patches of sharp goat-head stickers here and there along the street. We rest in the shade and let our feet cool off and sometimes we run most of way home to play whatever winds us up that afternoon.

We may be cowboys, other times we are fighting battles in the war we see on the newsreels or pretend we are cops and robbers.

We had just seen a movie where the robbers rode their horses up behind a passenger train, jumped on the caboose, climbed to the roof and ran along the top of the cars, jumping from one to the other. They reached the engine, overpowered the engineer, stopped and robbed the train.

We hurried home and on the way my brother Basil Jr. and our neighbor Lloyd and I planned to rob a train. The one my Dad had built in our yard, along the edge of the big ditch.

Our ideas of cowboy costumes were splendid. Our horses were the most beautiful, fastest and the very best that our imagination could provide. We were something very special in our own minds.

Like in the movie, we rode up to the last car of the train and found our first challenge. The row of rabbit hutches on the end of the train had a gap between them and the row of chicken coops and pens leading to the hen house, which was the engine. A large shade tree was in the gap and that really messed up the order of the railroad cars.

As always, when something was found to be out of whack, we simply pretended the problem didn't exist, went around it and climbed on the top of the coops and moved along the edges of the pens to reach the roof of the hen house.

We ran into our next challenge. Who was the engineer? One of us was changed from a robber to the engineer and the three of us were doing a pretend fight on the hen house. It was a confusing three-way tangle of pretend punches and knockdowns. It soon became evident that space on the hen house roof was too small for a proper robbery. I was bumped and fell backwards.

Pop had built a wire chicken pen off the side of the hen house and it sloped down into the big ditch and as I fell into a back swan dive, I looked down to see the hens scattering. Everything went black.

It felt dream-like sitting there with a growing knot on my forehead, out of breath, hurting too much to move and wondering what else might be wrong. My brother and Lloyd were already off the hen house and looking through the chicken wire, wide eyed with their mouths gaping. I guess I wasn't dead yet.

Normally, I would give those bastards a real good cuss'n out…but I was too whipped. The son-of-a-bitch that did this was yet to be identified. Maybe, it could've been my fault.

Basil unlatched and opened the pen gate and helped me out. We were all in deep trouble and the robbery was definitely a failure.

First we said nothing about my high dive off the hen house

into the ditch. We wondered how I would get over my sore neck. It hurt when I tried to move my head and I felt lousy.

Mom busted us when everyone said yes to a special treat but me. She took one look at me and saw the bump on my head and noticed the stiff way I turned to answer her. We completely spilled the beans, under mom's questioning.

Our doctor took x-rays, found no broken bones but did find something really weird. There was some worried whispering between the doctor and my folks then it was decided that nothing needed to be done. The Xray showed that under my left collar bone was an elbow joint on my top rib that connected to my second rib, which was twice as thick as the rest of the ribs. They called it a rib anomaly and has nothing to do with failed train robberies.

We found hot pads didn't help my stiff neck. I went back to school and after a while, figured I was just going to be a crippled third-grader who couldn't move his head to play ball or any thing else that I liked to do.

One Saturday we all piled into the car and drove over the Kettleman Hills, across the alkali flats to Hanford and Doctor Holmes, a chiropractor. He gave everyone in the family an adjustment. Mine was something else.

I had difficulty getting up on the table and it hurt my neck to move my head in any way. The doctor took my head in his hands and slowly moved it a little, rotating just slightly, then, snap. He jerked it to the right side but it didn't hurt any worse than before when I moved it a little bit.

He kneaded his way down my back, snapping and popping and back up to my neck, and jerked my head to the left side, again with no big pain. He did various adjustments, repeated the neck procedures and turned me loose with a pain free neck and a head that could rotate without pain. I was certain it was a miracle. I could do summersaults on the lawn in front of his office and everything.

We went back once more, a week later but the first time pretty much did the trick. No more being a crippled kid, no more robbing trains or excuses for dropping a ball or anything else. I was a lucky guy and life was damned good again.

3. DAD'S FAVORITE ROOSTER

LOTS OF things happen besides train robberies with the pens and the big ditch that make for good stories.

Two blocks south and across the ditch, Old Lady Wolf has a well kept house, yard and rows of organized pens of various sizes and kinds. She collects and raises shows birds, game birds, prized chickens and I don't know what else. I only know of her as a gray-haired lady who I see from a distance as she moves through her pens.

Most of our neighbors have chickens for meat and eggs. The Penningtons and the Hiedricks across the alley behind us, the Thompsons farther down the alley, the Uptons a block south of us and our next door neighbors the McFees all have chicken pens and some have rabbits for eating.

Pop must have done Mrs. Wolf some favor and in turn he was to receive one dozen special eggs that Dad planned to have hatched by his little bantam setting hen. I happened to ride in the car with Dad down to pick up the eggs.

There were only eleven eggs collected so Old Lady Wolf went to see if any more had been laid and found one more egg. It was still warm.

We headed back home and Pop put the eggs in a small pen with a shelter for the straw nest. Pop set the hen on the eggs and she checked them over and settled down to incubate them. We kept feed and water near the nest but the little hen never seemed to leave the warm eggs.

The little setting hen was in the last small pen along the ditch, before the tree and rabbit hutches. Pop marked the calendar for the hatch date, watched and waited. Good thing! The last warm egg never cooled so it hatched a day or two ahead of the rest.

Dad brought the chick inside and it was so soft and cute we couldn't keep our hands off of it. We all waited our turn at holding and petting it and telling it stories and stuff.

When the eggs had all hatched, we surrendered our chick to its stepmother and the other new chicks. The hen now had the run of the yard with her small brood and we were surprised to find one chick would run to us as the hen and other chicks would move away. We could still pick it up, pet it and tell it stuff.

The small flock was put in a pen after a couple weeks and

it became apparent that our pet was growing into a rooster. Dad would keep the hens for eggs and the roosters were headed for the frying pan. Except this time. We were going to have a new rooster for the hen house, when he was up to it.

When his time came he was gentle, big, beautiful, had fancy show bird parents and he was something special in the hen house.

Dad marks the calendar when litters of rabbits are due and the ages of various batches of young chickens so the table has a steady supply of meat for our family of five. And for our company who are always welcome even with the war on and all the meat rationed.

Sometimes, Dad gets day-old chicks from one of the stores in Hanford. He raises and sorts them in the various pens as they grow. The last stage for the young pullets comes when they are caught and dropped over the fence into the hen yard to replace the older less productive hens…who become stewing hens for our table.

Our pet rooster protected his flock and never bothered us while we collected eggs or changed the water and fed his hens. Even little brother Jesse could safely feed the hens. Life was good with us, with the chickens and the chores.

Dad was surprised and had to laugh when he dropped the first of a batch of new pullets over the fence in to the hen yard. The rooster had mounted the first young hen as it touched the ground and each time a new hen was caught and dropped over, the same thing happened and as the count climbed, the action remained swift. The last hen was covered about as quickly as the first.

Dad was so proud of his powerful pet rooster that he told the story on his weekend errands around town to just about every one he saw.

The next morning when Dad went out to check on his newly expanded flock, he was shocked to find a magnificent but dead young rooster on his back, under the roosting area. He really felt foolish for not knowing any better or being any smarter than the rooster about overdoing a good thing.

It was a sad day that pop buried our favorite young rooster and family pet, but as roosters go…could there have been any better way?

4. JESSE AND OUR CHICKENS

WE BOYS help Mom with the chores, when she keeps after us. Sometimes Jesse feeds the smallest young chickens, but he is so little the chickens quickly grow till they almost come up to his chest. Dad moves them up to the next holding pen when that happens.

Some of the young cocky roosters peck or jump up to spur Jesse while he tries to change their water, put mash in the feeders and throw out chicken feed for scratch.

One day we came to know the growing hostility Jesse was feeling toward the chickens and his thoughts of revenge.

Jesse had heard a particular expression many times. When that natural urge pressed him, a light went on in his head and a plan for revenge became clear to him.

Basil Jr. and I didn't notice Jesse unbutton his pants as he walked over to the chicken pen holding the ornery young birds. Apparently, to get a clear shot at those bad birds, he poked his weapon of revenge through the chicken wire and fired away. Piss on those bastards.

The next thing we heard was Jesse yelling bloody murder with tears streaming down his face. Mom came out of the house demanding to know what we had done to our little brother.

We all had to try to figure it out while Jesse cried in pain. Mom checked where and what Jesse was holding. What Mom found, was a bruised and pecked little boy's chicken shooter.

We could hardly keep a straight face as Mom put medicine and a tiny bandage on Jesse's battle wounded weapon.

Several times we have gotten cute fuzzy baby ducklings for Easter. We'd soon lose interest in them as they became fully-grown ducks and we'd forget our affection for them when they were served tasty and golden brown for dinner. With the war going on, meat and everything else was rationed and we ate better than a lot of kids.

It is common for a chicken or duck to lose their head to the axe on Sunday afternoons and get dressed for the dinner table. Rabbits get a sharp whack to the skull before losing their fur coat, which Pop stretches, dries and sells for just about enough money to pay for the rabbit feed. Smart deal.

Dad shoots the damned cats that come to hunt in our yard here on the edge of town. He shoots them with his twenty-two rifle. They come looking for small chickens and ducks, birds he has reserved for our diner table. Pop makes sure he gets a shot that can't travel…not the bullet nor the cat. Later, the cat *will travel* in a sack to the town dump.

We all keep an eye out for the little ducks and chickens that Pop sometimes lets run free in the yard to clean up weeds and bugs. Cats are the enemy.

Before dad built our new house, he built a garage and we lived in that for about two years while he was building our new house.

I remember a time when I was in the new garage we had moved into from our trailer house and was listening to stories and conversations with our company when Jesse came in and tugged at my arm. I didn't want to play outside while we had company and miss anything interesting but Jesse was persistent and determined to get me out there for something important.

Dad had laid a brick walk under our clotheslines and there on the bricks lay a dead cat and a dull axe. Jesse wasn't old enough to talk very well but he seemed to be concerned about the head not coming off to finish the job. I gave it a couple of chops but the dull axe just sort of mashed the dead cat's neck against the bricks.

I gave up and told Dad about the cat. Maybe he would know what to do.

No one, not the company, nor our folks, believed Jesse was big enough, or quick enough to have whacked the cat. They thought Basil Jr. or I had done it and for a joke…just said it was Jesse. Even years later I don't think my folks were ever really convinced Jesse could have been that quick or lucky with the axe.

My older brother and I did compound the gruesome incident. We were supposed to bury the cat but instead, we put the dead cat in a cracker box and put it across the big ditch in our neighbor's cellar on a shelf with jars of canned stuff.

It was a real dumb prank. We never heard how that joke played out but as time went by, we really felt bad about it and wished we had buried the cat. It was a bad deal…and not exactly the cat's meow.

5. MORE SHOOTING

I GUESS my older brother Basil Jr. was five and a half and I was about four years old when we were making roads with the edge of our hands and playing cars in our backyard and on our side of the big ditch.

At that time, we still lived in the small trailer with the room built next to it with a shed over the whole thing. My dad was about to build the new garage and the war hadn't started.

Across the ditch was a house that Piccolo Pete lived in with various characters, including two colorful parrots. I think Margaret Alexander, her parrots and the Painter were staying there when all hell broke loose in our mostly quiet neighborhood.

We heard some racket coming from across the ditch, the back screen door flung open and the Painter ran out in his white long-handled underwear. He had his clothes clutched under one arm, shoes in the other hand and was high-tailing it for the far corner of the shack.

Old Piccolo Pete stepped out, naked as a baby jay-bird, with his twenty-two-rifle and shot the hell out of the propane tank at the corner of the back porch as the Painter disappeared behind it and the corner of the house. The metal tank deflected the flying lead to I don't know where and the Painter was gone, until old Piccolo could cool off.

We sat frozen still, scared shitless about forty-feet away, hoping that crazy bastard wouldn't turn around and shoot us for seeing him naked, out there on his back porch…in plain daylight. He went back in without looking over our way.

Something weird was going on over there and Mom didn't want to talk about it, but she did say we were absolutely forbidden to go across the ditch. She didn't like what was going on over in that place.

That was the first time I remember anyone but my dad shooting a gun around there. But Dad just shot cats. The ones that came in our yard and hunted little chickens and ducks. I never saw where he kept it, but when a cat came around, Dad would appear with the twenty-two and another cat went to the dump.

Mom didn't like guns. She was shot with an empty gun when she was about twelve years old and living away up north in Novato. The shooter was a stupid asshole neighbor kid, who was plinking cans and things along the railroad tracks. When he thought he ran out of bullets, he started fooling around and threatening to shoot some of the kids.

He pointed the rifle at Mom and said, "Say your prayers Vivian, I'm going to shoot you." She turned her head away and a little to the side and said, "Please, don't shoot."

The bullet struck her in the neck, shattered her jaw and came out her cheek. I guess all hell broke loose when the kids heard the shot, saw all the blood and had to deal with getting help. Mom lost a lot of blood…almost too much.

A few doors down the block on Whitney Street, back in Avenal, my brother Basil was almost shot with another empty gun. Several kids were in a bedroom and one kid pulled out a twenty-two rifle and pointed it at my brother and said, "Basil, I think I'll just shoot you."

Roy Ethridge pushed the barrel away and said, "Don't ever point a gun at nobody." The gun fired into the wall, just as the kid was declaring that it was empty.

They all just looked at each other for a while. It seems as though no one could think of any thing to say that was worth a damn.

A few years later, it was Roy who got shot. Some of that same group were shooting rabbits and riding in an old pickup. Roy and some of the other guys, were standing in the truck bed and leaning against the cab with their arms resting on top to steady themselves as they looked for cottontails.

One of the kids in the cab had left their safety off and their rifle discharged when they hit a rut in the dirt road. The bullet went through the roof and Roy's arm. He was lucky it missed the bone and any major arteries. The ride to the hospital was quiet and the guilt of that foolish and grim mistake traveled with them far beyond that trip. Guns are made for killing...not something you should play around with...ever.

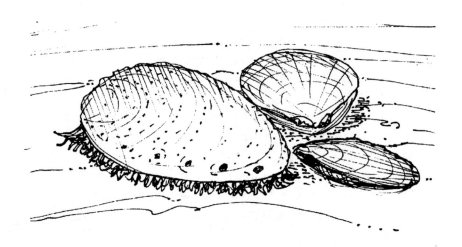

6. GETAWAYS TO THE COAST

SUMMERS can be hotter than hell in Avenal. So us smart people load up and go to the coast to cool off every chance we get. Pop likes to go to Cayucos best. He says the warm valley air comes through a mountain pass there and moves the fog out to sea when most of the rest of the coast is still fogged in.

I look forward to each trip we take to the coast and the adventures my Dad plans for us. And I never protest the wakeup calls two hours before dawn or question our parent's plans, no matter how outrageous they might seem. Our tribe will dress, load into the car and drive from Cayucos to a predetermined spot on the central California coast and be ready to hunt just before dawn like the Indians who gathered food along here in the olden days.

If clams are our prey, we usually drive south to Pismo

Beach and sometimes my brother and I will take turns holding the burlap clam bag for our Dad.

You can expect the chill of the cold and foggy morning to soak into your bones and the icy water to finish the job. The bag limit is ten each and Pop sees to it that we all get our share of legal clams.

His gray sweat shirt, blue jeans, and black tennis shoes get soaked in the choppy surf as he probes the sand for clams with his fork. When he locates what might be a clam, he scoops it up on his fork and lets the water wash away the sand exposing the prize. Dad checks the size and sacks those clams that don't pass through the clam gage. The shorts are reburied or opened and eaten raw on the spot. Some clam diggers carry a small jar of mustard in their shirt pocket and snack as they work for their limit.

Our Dad and his Dad, when he comes along with us, will always open some clams to eat raw. I was very small when I joined in this ritual and didn't realize at the time that these creatures were alive as I chewed and swallowed them. Up north, I eat raw oysters with my Dad and other Grandpa Hiribarren. Older brother Basil Jr. is too sophisticated to be drawn into eating live animals.

Us hunters change into dry clothes and head back to our hunting camp. Dad shells the clams and helped Mom run them, along with onions, celery, soda crackers and seasonings, through the meat grinder for baked clam on the half shell to be served after the hot clam chowder.

These delicious meals, fresh from the sea, are rewards for rising early, enduring discomfort and staying the course.

The early mornings that we pile into the car and head up north, mean we are going to be abalone hunting above Cambria and only Dad will get really wet. He wades in the tide pools feeling underwater in crevices and under ledges for large red abalone.

Sometimes Pop has to hold his breath when the ocean surge washes over him as he works to get leverage and pry loose an abalone that is just out of reach beneath the rise and fall of the water's surface at low tide.

The smaller more abundant black abalone is found in crevices and hiding places on the exposed rocks above the water's surface. We use a tire iron to pry the abalone loose from their strong hold on the rock.

The bag limit is ten and the minimum size is seven inches for reds and five inches for blacks. Pop hunts to get some reds and we fill out our limits with the blacks.

He changes into dry clothes, runs the car heater and sometimes he's still shaking after driving back down the coast to Cayucos.

Dad shells, trims and slices the abalone into steaks and just before dinner he pounds the steaks to tenderize them. Mom cooks the abalone in a very hot skillet for about fifteen seconds on each side. On a good year, when weather and tides are right, we have both clam and abalone dinners.

A couple times Dad collected some deeper water mussels at low tide and Mom steamed and served them swimming in hot butter and minced garlic. He also collected some ocean snails and put them in a box with a thin layer of cornmeal for them to eat and stuff themselves during the night. Mom steamed and served them with hot minced garlic and butter.

We catch lots of snappers off the Cayucos pier, when they are running in July and August, and they are good for fish fries. The Cayucos pier is where I had my first experience with something like fly-fishing. We use snapper jigs with four to six colorful yarn-wrapped hooks and a small weight at the bottom of the rig. There is no messy bait for us to fool with.

Schools of small fish hang out under the kelp growing on the old pilings that support the pier. We catch some perch, but most are a juvenile fish we call snappers. Sometimes schools of small anchovies migrate into the area and are hunted by jack smelt and mackerel, making the action wild with the bigger aggressive fish hitting our light rigs.

I crank the rig down near the kelp, jig, crank down more, jig and on down to the bottom. Then I crank and jig back up to the surface. If you count the cranks, you can figure the depth of the school and catch fish as the jigging action excites them to chase the colorful yarn flies. Once you have a fish on, it is common to catch several before reeling them in and putting them in the half-filled bucket of water.

One of our other sources of fresh prey from the ocean is deep-sea fishing-trips. Pop had ordered a bamboo ocean rod and star drag saltwater reel from the Sears catalog for seventeen dollars. On his first boat trip with the new outfit he won the seventeen-dollar jackpot and paid for his new deep sea fishing gear.

My brother and I were too young to fish on our first deep-sea trip. We stayed in the old Cayucos campground and Dad cooked breakfast over a fire in the cold, damp early morning darkness. We walked out on the pier to the stairs leading down to the landing and boarded the sport fishing boat.

The skipper headed for the fishing grounds under the cover of fog and later we saw the sun burn through the gray stuff about noon. Dad caught fish, we all had lunch and my older brother lost his lunch to the fish and had a rough trip. I gloated over my good fortune to survive without throwing up and being such a fine sailor and all.

Pop was disappointed on our return trip to Avenal when

the first thing Mom heard out of my mouth was that Basil Jr. got sea sick and I didn't. She was horrified that the poor little guy was stuck on the ocean for a miserable boat trip. It made Pop's camping and fishing adventure with his two older boys, sound like a disaster while it really was a memorable experience...from my point of view.

Sometimes when it gets hot around here, I daydream of the ocean and travel in my mind to the cool breezes of Cayucos. It's a good deal.

7. THE LAST OF GRAMMAR SCHOOL

IT IS GREAT to finally be an eight-grader. I ride my old rebuilt bike to school and all the little kids think we are big stuff. My teacher is the best one I've ever had in school so far.

Miss Wash is so smart and she can handle the biggest kids like Jimmy Tinsley and Bert Wayner. Even they like her and quiet down when she says so. She thinks I can do better in school than I have in the past and gets me to study more.

She even got me to work more carefully on the big poppy poster contest for the war veterans. She says I will be an artist when I grow up. It's the first time I have won anything in classroom work or got my picture in the big valley paper. Of course I always win the playground chinning-event in my group, starting way back in the fifth grade, but you don't have to be smart to do that

Burl Young and I are on Coach Lang's tumbling team. We are good at walking on our hands and take turns setting and breaking the distance record for our school.

Next year I will be a freshman in high school and all the bigger kids will look down on me, so I'd better enjoy the eight-grade while I'm a big shot. It took a long time to get here and it wasn't always much fun.

In kindergarten, I fell asleep in the sandbox several times. No one told the teacher and she never missed me. One of the times I woke up in the sandbox, the playground was deserted. As I walked around the building, I saw all the kids lined up to get on the bus and those bastards were going to go home without me.

To make things worse, Phyllis Cass would always beat me to the letter P in the circle of alphabet letters and plop her stinky butt on it during story time. The F sounding name getting to sit on the letter P ruined my start in school.

The other thing I hated was when Mom made me wear those little-kid bib pants to school. I would tuck in the bib and tie the shoulder straps around my waist. No real cowboys who rode horses ever wore bib pants. I wanted to get a good start on being a real cowboy.

The first-grade was no better. My folks waited until school was about to start and then decided to have Basil's and my tonsils and adenoids taken out. They didn't worry me with the fact that I would also be circumcised.

My folks thought it was funny when I woke up and needed to pee. After I peed, I asked the lady nurse, "When you had your tonsils out, did it hurt when you peed?"

I was a week late, sore, wearing a bandage and out of step with my first-grade class-work. I was also put in a special speech group to correct letter sounds I was getting wrong. The Fs and the Ps were still giving me trouble.

Never do a favor for a neighbor kid without asking what is involved. In the second grade, Charles Cass asked me to meet him after school by the kindergarten swings. He refused to say why.

Well, he shows up and tells me to whistle if I see anybody coming. He says he is going in to get the milk money while I wait. He goes away and a kid comes walking by and I give the whistle a try…nothing happens. Charles never asked me if I could whistle. He comes out and we go about three blocks to a little store and Charles wants to change a mess of nickels and dimes into quarters. He gets about four and I get about three-quarters that I don't know what to do with or how to explain. The money was a big problem but I never got caught and Charles found out I was of little value to him as a look-out.

I was a cripple for a while in the third grade after the failed train robbery and the back dive into the ditch, which was a real son-of-a-bitch.

We play different games that can get us in trouble when things get out of control and some one gets mad or messes up. Marbles and milk bottle caps are games you can win off other kids or you can be the loser. Fudging and cheating cause trouble.

We make stuff that get us in trouble, like using straws to shoot spit wads or rigging up clothes pins to shoot match sticks with the metal springs to fire the sticks. I shot a matchstick into a kid's ice cream cone after lunch. It was a good shot and it stuck right in the cone.

He told the teacher and she made me empty my pockets and took the clothes pin gun, the spare parts and all my matchsticks. She said she was going to keep an eye on me and I had better not bring anymore stuff like that to school. I was lucky the principal didn't give me some swats.

At home, we make rubber guns with clothespins for a trigger release to grab one end of the rubber from the back of the grip and stretch the strip of car inner tube over the front end of a thin piece of wooden board for the barrel. You squeeze the pin and the rubber flings off the end and out at the target. With two pens, you can have a two-shot gun.

Things in school weren't going too well for me until I got to the fifth grade. I won the May Day chinning event in my group and set a new record with seventeen underhanded chin-ups.

That was also the year we were marched out on the front lawn by the flagpole, saluted the flag and sang God Bless America. Those German nazi bastards had surrendered. Then, a little later we whipped old Tojo and his Japs. Our boys were coming home...heroes!

Our neighbor, Leroy Hugo, four houses to the east, lost his legs to a German land mine over seas, as he was following a tank and fighting for us in the war. Some others didn't come back home to hear our thanks. Some who are shell shocked, like Eddie and Fuzzy don't fully understand how proud we are of them. Well, maybe Fuzzy had some problems before the war. Anyway, there was a high price paid to stop Hitler and Tojo from getting to us at home in Avenal.

Every year on the last day of school before Christmas vacation, we have a party, then march single file to the picture show for a special Christmas program. Santa wears his best red suit and hands each of us a candy-cane, hard candy, an orange, all in a colored mesh sack. Then...no school until after New Years!

Mr. Davis was my fifth grade teacher and my first teacher who wasn't a woman. He wasn't mean or anything. I drew a picture of him once while he was talking and someone told on me. I thought I was a goner, but he looked at it, smiled and kept it. He said it was good. Other than mom, he was my first fan.

We also had a visit from one of our friend's dad, who was a big shot up at Standard Oil. Mr. Gail Carbiener told us about the oil field and how it got started with the deepest oil well ever drilled and how the oil was down there in a sort of cave like a barrel and had lots of natural gas in with it. The town had to be named and built for all the oil workers and new business people who were moving here.

That explained why people came from all over the country to live in Avenal. It had jobs that paid good money when there weren't any extra jobs in those other places around America.

Someone asked Mr. Carbiener how long it would take to pump that barrel kind of deal dry and he said about twenty years. The kid said, "Then what?" Mr. Carbiener told us not to worry...we'd be out of school by then.

We moved up the ditch. Mom didn't get along with the nosey neighbors so Pop bought a little place up the ditch and sold our new house and he is going to build a new one farther out with no close nosey neighbors.

This little old place on the dead end of Yosemite is like camping out, but it will just have to do until Pop builds us the new one. My bedroom has a chest and a place to hang clothes along the wall as you come in the door and turn left down a walkway between two metal bunk beds. Us three boys sleep on the bunks and so does Grandpa Perry, when he comes back to visit from the coast.

Grandpa didn't like the valley heat and family bickering so Pop sold his little place and bought him a cabin in Cayucos. Grandpa can walk about four blocks and find any thing he needs, like groceries and wine. He fishes off the pier for snappers and surf-perch. Basil and I are big enough to stay with Grandpa for a week or two during the summer. We take turns so he has more company, but not too much.

Mom and Dad sleep in the front room next to our bunkroom. It has the chrome dinette-set, their bed, a big chair, a dresser, a little heater and the front door to a small porch. There is a bathroom with a tub and wash basin next to the kitchen. The kitchen is big enough for a walkway between the sink, counter and stove along the outer wall with the refrigerator and storage shelves along the opposite wall.

The back door opens to the kitchen and you go past the refrigerator and turn right to enter the living room. The edge of our folk's bed serves as a couch for more places to sit.

We've all been camping here for several years now and the adventure of it wore off sometime back.

But something neat happened at school that made me feel real good…with out getting killed. Jimmy Tinsely, who is the toughest kid in school, pushed me, or something and I put up my dukes and moved around him like I was ready to duke it out with him. Jimmy was surprised and maybe a little amused at the scrawny little kid acting like he was ready to fight.

Well, the teacher was right there to break up a fight that never happened. I was sent to the principal's office for a semi fight. I was chewed out real good and Jimmy got some swats. I secretly felt that I caused the most damage without landing a blow. I am not sure if I was the winner, but I felt good, while Jimmy could have really punched the daylights out of me.

I think it was in the seventh grade that my friend Lloyd did some weird things. He is a smart straight-A student, but he still does weird things like trying to fly…twice.

The first time he broke his arm. He showed me the scraps of rope tied to a post and he told me about the bamboo frame he covered with bed-sheets all sewn to make a huge kite deal. He waited for a windy day and his buddies held the kite until he was set for take off. Lloyd said the tail wasn't long enough because the thing went up and looped on take-off, it flung him away and broke his arm.

I would've liked to been there to see it. Years ago, he got to see my stupid back dive off the hen house into the big ditch during our failed train robbery.

His second flight was a real humdinger. He reworked the kite and he and his gang carried it across town and up into Kettleman Hills. Lloyd said he picked a hill facing the stiff wind and got set to hang on and glide off into the sky. He told his buddies to let go and he took off like a son-of-a-bitch with the ground falling away beneath him.

I said Lloyd was smart and he quickly calculated the drop off, speed, downward angle, he let go and dropped. In that short time he still fell twenty or thirty feet onto a steep and muddy hillside for a very forgiving landing.

Farther out, it was a couple hundred feet drop at the lowest spot before the rise of the next hill. The flying machine had picked up a lot of speed before it crashed into the next hill about a hundred feet from the top. Lloyd was smart enough to let go in time to save his ass serious injury or death.

My Dad's Mom was a Cessna who had a couple of uncles who built the Cessna airplane. Dad's Grandpa Huffman's family lived in Ohio where the Wright Brothers did some flying at Huffman Prairie Flying Field. Lloyd would've fit in with that wild bunch of early flying adventurers.

Another daredevil stunt Lloyd pulled was the time he decided to set a distance record with a bike jump across the big ditch.

Lloyd's bike wasn't much and we thought he would break it up if he rode it off into the ditch. He said he wanted to see how far out he could go at top speed. Well, he gets a full speed run at it and lands half way across the ditch, in the deepest part. To our surprise, him and the bike are both OK. Two more jumps to the same spot convinces him that it is the best he can do and he survives with his bike not much worse for the wear. No one else wanted to challenge Lloyd's wild and crazy record setting jumps.

While I am doing pretty good in the eighth grade Lloyd is getting all As. He asks me to come by his trailer house where he lives with his dad, two sisters and his granny. He wants me to see an oil painting he is working on. The oil painting is of an old Indian. It is so damned good that I am really stunned. I thought I was the best artist, but I don't know anything about oil painting. He says he is reading about some old time artists and taking oil painting lessons.

Lloyd is the weirdest goddamned kid I have ever seen in Avenal or heard of…but he is absolutely the best kind of weird anyone could be. He gives us Okies a good name.

8. THE ROAD TO DEVIL'S DEN

THERE'S no way around it. It is greedy dreams of big money that put us boys on a road to the Devil's Den. Raising spending money is no easy task in a small oil town where people work hard for a dollar and hang on to it real tight, unless they happen to be thirsty.

Well, that's where we get 'em. We take our bikes and gather bottles they throw away along the roads leading out of Avenal, turn them in and collect the loot. Each year before school is out, we begin our treasure hunt to pay for our summer pass to the Avenal swimming pool. During hot days, the Avenal swimming pool is the best place a kid can spend his afternoons. And on Saturdays we head home, eat and go to the theater for the evening show.

This bottle scavenging works out pretty good about once a year. To get more loot, we have to work some new territory.

I guess that's how someone came up with the idea of collecting bottles all the way down the highway to Devil's Den, cashing in the loot at the little store and gas station by the labor camp and riding our bikes back up to Avenal.

Brother Basil Jr. and I had gone down there with our neighbors, the Hodgson family to pick cotton several times for Christmas money. There were rows of twelve by twelve, one room wooden shacks with a water faucet for every six or so of them. Somewhere, there must have been some toilets but I never saw them.

We were startled one morning while we were waiting in the Hodgson's car, just before daylight, to pick cotton. A ruckus broke out in one of the little shacks and a small pudgy balding guy in his underwear was flung out the door and a slender guy came out after him.

Every time the pudgy guy got up, the slender guy punched him and knocked him down. The guy getting the hell beat out of him said he didn't care how much the other guy hit him, he would always love Evelyn. The slender guy lost interest and Evelyn came out to comfort the pudgy guy. And pretty soon, they all went back into the small shelter.

Picking cotton didn't work out for me worth a damn. I didn't make but a couple dollars because of being slower than molasses and easily bored.

The whole shebang is called Devil's Den. Maybe, because of the tough times and the kind of humor that desperate folks need to survive. Some might even think it is little more than a hellhole for lost souls.

My brother Basil Jr. and I and our neighbors Howard and Myron Hodgson decided to give the Devil's Den trip a go. We started out early and rode down town and onto the highway and then south toward our fortune.

On the road outside town we found pickings were slim, maybe because of competitive scavenging. We figured that as we peddled out further, business would pick up and we'd get into the real money.

We picked up bottles here and there, some were strange to us but bottles are bottles and we kept working our way down the road. By the time we got to Devil's Den, we were tired, thirsty and our sacks were light on bottles. Maybe some one was scavenging bottles out there where money was scarce too.

Our get rich plan was in serious trouble and soon got worse. Most of the bottles were not ones they carried at the little store and the few that were all right were dirty. The old guy working there was disgusted and impatient with us when he found we had no money to spend in the store.

Near the gas pumps was a hose used for filling radiators and we all took a drink for the ride home. The hot water tasted of sun baked old rubber hose.

We immediately discovered something that should have been obvious. A detail we had totally overlooked, mainly, because we were focused on scooping up bottles and turning them to big money.

Peddling our heavy old balloon tired bikes back up the road was much more difficult because we were worn down and hot. But worse yet, the road up the narrow valley actually was slightly up hill for about eighteen miles.

This bad news, added to our recent financial disaster, and fatigue was pretty defeating as we slowly peddled toward our distant home.

We didn't carry watches, water or anything else of use on such a trip. The sun told us it was getting mid afternoon and towards the hottest part of the damned day.

We would peddle for a while and then walk for a while up and down the slight gentle rises and dips toward home as the day wore on. We were getting desperate. The road stretched on into the unknown distance and we just wanted to be home. We were tired and thirsty, hungry and getting a little scared.

At our lowest moment, our asses dragging, when we thought we just couldn't make it much further, a truck came in to view and we started waving madly. The truck slowed as it passed and then stopped. It was a big flat bed rig running empty.

The driver asked what the problem was and we told him we were worn out and couldn't make it much further. We needed a ride.

The driver wasn't supposed to take passengers, but it turned out that he was Buster May's dad, Blackie, and he said he'd give us a ride to the edge of town if we didn't tell anybody.

We threw our bikes on the flatbed trailer and piled into the cab for a crowded but wonderful ride to the edge of town. Peddling and walking that last mile up the sloping Kettleman Plain across town seemed like it took forever.

All thoughts of lost fortunes and shit-house plans were left behind us on the road to Devil's Den.

And I think that was the first time I was desperately happy to be back home again, in Avenal.

9. HUNTING OUR DESERT FUNGUS

WHEN THE rain stops and sunshine breaks through the gray skies, we know the conditions are right for something special to make an appearance. Sometimes we walk the short distance or drive to the edge of town and begin our traditional hunt for Avenal truffles. You know…mushrooms.

Mom prefers the unopened buttons because they stay

clean and don't have creepy bugs yet. We can be choosy since they're usually plentiful…much more than we can use.

I like to scan and study the ground for a slightly lifted cracked area that conceals a small mushroom starting to expand, yet not open, before changing from a pink to a brown underside and before being invaded by bugs

I locate the center of the radiating cracks, push my knife into the ground a couple inches out from the center of the cracked and rising earth, pry down and lift. Up out of the crumbling dirt comes the prey only to be taken captive. I carefully brush it off, trim the stem and place the prize in a shallow box. We often use a box as a tray to keep them face down to stay clean.

We hunt the open patches in the sagebrush covering the Kettleman Plain surrounding the town. Sometimes we retrace our steps to find more mushrooms where we have just dug several minutes earlier. They seem to each be on different time clocks and puff up on their own schedule like popcorn without the pop.

There are all kinds of mushrooms, puffballs and toadstools. If you try, you probably can't find a poison one. But we only take the smooth white mushrooms with the pink underside. Over the years, we never have had a bad mushroom.

Mom and Pop were born and grew up in northern California where some people collected all kinds of mushrooms and were serious and competitive food collectors. Pop says about once every few years or so he would read about a family that was poisoned, after a lifetime of eating every thing they could lay their hands on.

We take no such chances and dine on fresh mushrooms in season with confidence that our names will not appear in a sad news story.

Mom runs water in the kitchen sink, puts the mushrooms in to float, to drop sand and dirt that might be clinging to them. She carefully washes each mushroom and lays them face down to drain and dry. At mealtime she slices them into a pan, adds some freshly minced garlic, seasons and sautés them in butter and serves them with dinner.

Mom learned to prepare unusual dishes from her father who was a French chef on an ocean liner that sailed out of San Francisco to the Hawaiian Islands. He would prepare family dinners for the holidays and other special meals. And at one time, had a restaurant, bar, hotel and livery stable in Navato, just north of San Francisco.

Mom prepares and serves, at different times, what I think are tasty dishes like kidney sauté, tripe, frog legs, clam on the half shell, mussels, snails, abalone, pickled pigs feet and sliced tongue. Of course, I started eating this stuff before I could talk or really know what I was eating. So collecting and eating mushrooms does not seem odd or alarming, just something we do.

We always hope for a timely rain to bring fresh mushrooms to collect and serve for holiday dinners. They are good deals because they are free, too.

10. THE BLACK MOUNTAIN BIKE RIDE

I LIKE BEING a freshman in high school. Even though I am not a big shot anymore, I am bigger. And I have more freedom to walk or ride my bike all around the place. It's a better deal.

When I look west from Avenal, across the narrow valley to the hills and Tar Canyon, the biggest thing I see is the long and tall Black Mountain. Maybe it was only a matter of time but one day us kids got the idea to ride our bikes into the hills and up as high as we could go and maybe climb big old Black Mountain…at least one time.

The Sagasters, O'Dales and Larreas have ranches up that

way somewhere and their kids all ride the bus to school down here in Avenal.

We went over our bikes, oiled the coaster brakes, chain, checked the air in the tires and packed a lunch for an early morning start. We've learned to plan better since that screwed up Devil's Den disaster. How dumb could you be?

There would be five riders going, my brother Basil Jr. and I, our neighbors, Willie and Howard Hodgson and Bud Hudson. We were all riding old bikes that were pretty sorry, had welded places and were a mix of scrap parts and new parts.

At first light we gathered by the big ditch on Dome St. and peddled down and across town to Highway 33, rode to the cut off and up into the hills. We walked our bikes up the steepest part of the hills and rode fast down them and up the next hill as far as we could go. Then we'd walk again.

The spring weather was mild, the grass green and here and there, were splashes of wildflower colors. We passed grazing cattle and some ranches nestled in the hills as the road curved its way up toward the big mountain.

When we came to a private gate our plans changed. Black Mountain was over a few more hills, back out of reach and on someone's ranch.

We decided to climb to the top of a big hill on the right side of the road and eat our lunch under an oak tree that was standing up there. The view we found was a surprise. Our lunch under the tree was above all the hills leading up to it.

We could see over the tops of the green hills to the valley below and across to our town at the foot of the Kettleman Hills. All under a clean blue sky, decorated with big white clouds. Our adventure was splendid, far beyond our expectations.

Most of the ride down and out of the hills was easy going.

Willie was the oldest and led the way, winding down toward the valley. I guess we got used to the unusually fast speed we could generate down hill and we were braking less and beginning to fly as the hills looked easier.

There was some talking with Bud and then Basil yelled, "My chain's jumped and I have no brakes. I can't stop."

Next thing I know, Basil shoots by me and rolls on toward Howard like a bat out of hell and everyone is yelling. Oh Shit!

It looked like my brother was in some dangerous trouble. He gained speed on down the winding road. The great adventure was turning sour.

I guess old Willie was thinking a mile a minute. He rides up a steep cut-bank, brakes to a sliding stop, hops off and runs back down to the road and faces the runaway cyclist.

We don't know if Willie ever saw any movies of bullfighters, but that day he faced something that was going much faster than a bull's charge.

Like a matador, Willie positioned himself, but instead of letting the bull pass, he grabs the horns to stop the bull.

All hell broke loose. Basil flies over the handlebars and rolls down the road leaving some skin smeared along the blacktop. Willie gets the worst of it. The force rips him off his feet and flings him and the bike into a pile with the horn goring him in the crotch.

Actually, the handlebar didn't quite gore him. It was too blunt and was covered with a soft rubber grip. Willie rolled around in pain long after Basil gathered himself up and walked back to the pileup to retrieve his bike.

Basil twisted the handlebars around so they were square to the front tire and put the chain back on the sprockets. Finally, Willie got back on his bike and led us the rest of the way home.

Sometimes I wonder if he suffers any lasting impairment from his bull fighting injury. I think Willie is, perhaps, Avenal's first and bravest matador.

11. THE OLD DECOMPOSER

JAKE IS AN honorary Uncle who stands out among the characters in an oil town like Avenal.

He's tall, slender and bald, which makes him look much older than his years, to us kids.

Some oil workers like Jake, who are divorced or bachelors, become permanent fixtures in the Standard Oil Company's bunkhouse above the town in the Kettleman Hills, which appears to grow a forest of oil derricks.

Apparently, the price is right for the bunkhouse, the routine is simple and a man can have a little more spending money by staying there.

Jake is always welcome at our house and he will have himself over for dinner often, bringing some groceries from Finster's Market and a bottle from Rice's liquor store. Both places are just a few blocks over on Skyline Blvd.

He teases us kids and tells us we have to learn to take it as well as dish it out. When we get mad and cuss the son-of-a-bitch out...he just grins. And wins.

There is that saying...sticks and stones may break my bones...but names will never hurt me. Well...don't ever let anyone get your goat that way.

Mom cooks dinner, we all eat our meal and the bottle empties through the course of the evening. Jake recites racy limericks, poems, sings old songs and new Hank Williams honky-tonk tunes. I guess he likes the family company for a change and the evening might cost him less than a meal in a restaurant and drinks in a bar. And he gets a cussing out, now and then.

Later in the evening, old Jake sometimes sings his more humorous version of popular songs. He will introduce these songs by saying, "Here's a song I decomposed myself."

Various topics of conversation come up for examination, some of a more serious nature. Jake is intelligent, well read, creative and a free thinker. He has seen first hand the sweatshops exploiting desperate and powerless workers, the excesses of the callous rich and he is aware of rampant political corruption.

Unions look to Jake like the answer to a common man's dream of gaining respect and dignity. And the idea of redistributing wealth, seems like a fair and good idea, from where he stands. In fact, these conditions suggest to Jake that communism is better than the cruel capitalistic system that keeps the common man poor.

Pop takes the Valley's daily paper, a Sunday San Francisco paper, the Sunday Los Angeles Times plus four or five national magazines and he reads best selling books. Dad has some powerful opposing answers for Jake and the discussions are a work in progress through more than a few bottles from Rice's liquor store.

It was my Dad's interest in baseball that brought Jake back from the grip of communism. At first, Jake said the players all played the same nine innings and should get equal pay for equal time. When Dad got Jake hooked on Willie Mays, baseball and winning, Jake discovered baseball statistics.

Jake found some hitters drive in more runs, some players make fewer errors and some pitchers give up fewer hits and runs resulting in more wins. After all was considered, Jake concluded that not all players are of equal value to a team's success.

To Jake's disappointment, some union leaders were connected to the Mafia and doing prison time for looting pension funds, tax evasion and general corruption.

Maybe most of the good guys play ball.

When my older brother Basil Jr. got his drivers license, Jake found a willing driver for his occasional short trips to see his sister down the road in Taft.

While Junior loves to drive Jake's Ford, the price becomes a little too steep at times for a self-conscious teenager. Yet, my brother is too respectful to say much to Uncle Jake. That is assumed to be pretty much out of the question.

When it is mealtime on a trip, Junior hates to admit to being hungry because that means cafes and waitresses.

Jake loves to sing to waitresses. He knows they have to

listen if they are going to get a tip. And my brother feels like crawling under his plate when Jake launches into the popular Hank Williams tune, "Hey, good lookin', whatcha got cookin'? How about cookin' somethin' up with me?"

After the meal, the bill and the tip, Jake sings for his parting song more Hank Williams, "I got a hot rod Ford and a two dollar bill and I know a spot just over the hill. The music is good and the dancing is free. If you want to have fun come along with me."

I suppose, over the years, Jake, being the ham he is, has hit most all of the cafes and bars between Avenal and Taft on one trip or another. Junior, by his count, thinks he's been on far too many of those trips.

Maybe Jake is the most unusual and fun thing that has happened on that day to some of the people in little cafes who see this smiling old man singing like he was in a musical.

A tired, bored and under paid waitress might be flattered to have old Jake sing to her. Hey, in movies guys break out singing any old time they want. Jake probably knows that most ordinary people don't mind his singing, his jokes or his stories.

At our house, Jake plays to a receptive audience before, after and sometimes during dinner. We seldom wonder what anyone might think...and we are learning to laugh when someone tries to get our goat.

I enjoy the sight of that old son-of-bitch's smiling face, sense of humor, life lessons and all those songs.

Decomposed or not.

12. FRESHMAN UPS AND DOWNS

OUR FRESHMAN English assignment is to write a nomination speech for one of the candidates for student body offices. While I can make my Fs and P sounds properly, I think that "Phyllis" thing in kindergarten messed up my spelling and my writing still suffers. And I wonder about that brain scrambling back-dive off the engine of our train and landing on my head in the big ditch.

From kids comments and things my aunts up by San Francisco say, I have absorbed an Okie drawl from all my best friends. Speeches aren't my deal either.

For the class assignment, I'm picking out Bill Lyles, who is a classmate of Basil and is running for student body vice president.

Bill's dad has a pipeline company, which makes him a rich kid in Avenal…something you don't want to be in a small town of regular, working folks.

An undefined resentment or jealousy can be cruel when wielded by children or anyone else for that matter. Basil told me Bill would plan different ways to run home after grammar school, to escape the bigger bullies who loved to humiliate anyone available for any imagined reason.

Well, they just made him the best damn miler on the high school track team. Bill plays football and basketball too. He's a poor target to mess with now.

They will still needle him, when they get the chance. Basil said they were on a bus trip up north for a game and someone asked what was growing in the big fields flooded with water. No one could guess, then Bill said it was rice. Well, someone laughed and said this was California not China…Dumb ass.

When things moved on to other banter, Basil asked him if that really was rice. Bill said they had plenty of water up there and it was a good place to grow a lot of rice.

I never saw him run track or heard the crowd roar as Bill came running down the final sprint to win a race with cheers ringing in his ears.

I was in the stands at a basketball game with the clock ticking down to the buzzer, the fans chanting shoot. Shoot. Shoot. Bill launched the ball from half court and as the ball arched toward the basket, the crowd roared and when it banked through the hoop, the place just exploded. He must have smiled to himself as well as the crowd.

Bill gets around more than most of us, but he sometimes pays for all of his extra experiences and knowledge by getting rudely ribbed. He does get back by doing some outstanding things.

I'm trying to write a funny decomposition of an article that I read in the new issue of Reader's Digest.

The Digest story is a short essay on what a boy is and all the funny things he does and what you find in his pockets and places you might find him doing odd things...all adding up to be a real boy, but not serious campaign speech material.

Miss Smith liked my decomposed version as a nomination speech, shows it to Bill Lyles, he agrees to have me deliver it in front of the student body assembly for real...and then she tells me I have to do it. I am petrified and say no way.

Well, she tells me I will do it. When I do, the whole place cracks up all the way through it. I am not sure if they are just laughing at me and my Okie drawl or the words but I finish it and Bill comes out on stage grinning at me. I don't know what that is all about either. I hope he doesn't plan to kick my butt.

Miss Smith says I did a good job and Bill wins his race for student body vice president. Every thing is working out just fine and dandy.

A few days later Miss Smith stops me in the hall and is furious with me. Her eyes are wide and watery as she asks me how I could do such a thing to her. It seems that someone read the Reader's Digest essay and told Mrs. Smith I had stolen it for the speech and it was a big scandal on us.

I wonder if Jake could help me explain to her about how decomposing stuff works, because I feel like I'm back in kindergarten, somehow missing the damned bus. This is a screwed-up deal.

Our math teacher, Mr. Halley is just about everybody's favorite teacher in the whole high school, even though all the math classes are very hard work.

My art teacher, Mr. Russell is a real artist and is teaching me about perspective, light and shadow, composition and color. I'm doing OK because there is no spelling to get marked down on. Art is good.

We are all mixed together in art class, freshmen like me to seniors like Bob Ballard. There aren't many artists in high school so some kids are doing crafts like leather purses, wallets or belts. Mr. Russell teaches us what ever we want to sign up to learn.

Sometimes I get to go outside and draw different stuff with Bob. He is so good at drawing everything. I can't believe it. He is good at sports too. And Bob's folks have a black Lincoln Continental with the covered tire on the back…it is the best car there is.

I go out for all the sports, but I sit on the bench a lot. Ninety-five pounds does not make for a very scary football player. I am also short but slow. The main thing is to keep a C average to be eligible to play sports, which is the best thing about going to high school.

The best thing about summer is no school, the swimming pool, evening ballgames, vacations on the coast and the YMCA camp at Sequoia Lake. Basil and I have been going across the valley and up to Camp Redwood since I was nine years old. First it was two weeks then it got shortened to ten days but it's still so great. We have the biggest redwood trees in the world up there. You can't even believe it when you see them.

13. OUR SANDLOT BASEBALL

BASEBALL HAS always been around Avenal as far back as I can remember. Or, at least playing catch at school or home has always been here. We play catch to pass the time. It is good and it's still free. We play for hours sometimes when we don't have to go in for dinner or something else.

We get on teams and play in the summer, before the evening men's softball games and in our spare time we play in vacant lots near our house. When we play with Pop, he lets us in on secrets and tricks of the game. He knows all kinds of stuff you never heard of.

Pop can throw a knuckle ball that kind of flutters and is hard to catch and even harder to hit. He can throw curve balls and change ups that will really mess up your swing.

And he showed us how to bunt. It's like reaching out to catch the ball with the bat in your hand. You can't miss…if you can catch a ball.

Kids hate to catch a bad throw when it is low. It can bounce up and hit you in the legs or worse. A low throw is scary.

Well, Pop showed me how to scoop up those low throws like they were nothing. You just imagine the ball bouncing up at the same angle as it comes in and you scoop on the spot you think it will be. It works and makes you look like a pro. I haven't passed along that one and it gives me an edge at playing first base.

Maybe being small, the coaches seem to be overlooking my good glove and strong arm. But it could be my hitting has suffered from lack of batting practice. Pop said he wasn't much of a hitter either.

The whole secret of baseball is keeping your eye on the ball. To catch it, hit it and know what it is going to do or where it will go when it is hit. You watch it hit your glove, hit your bat and hit the target you are throwing to. And you have to know where to throw the ball…before the next play starts.

Well, Pop loves baseball and somehow him and Floyd Rice cooked up a deal for Pop to put together an older kids softball team and coach it for the summer. They named it The Rice's Cubs for Pop's favorite team and our closest liquor store. We have nifty maroon uniforms with gold lettering and trim.

Pop ran up a phone bill scheduling games for the team

and passed it along to Floyd. Pop also burned up a lot of gas with Floyd's furniture store delivery truck, hauling players all over hell to win a lot of games that summer for old Floyd Rice, us kids and Pop. Mollie Rice paid the bills.

But, one summer cured Floyd of being a big spending ball team owner. Uniforms, bats and balls, telephone bills and gas...well, maybe Pop had put one over on him. Floyd continued to sponsor many other things, but not for Pop.

I don't think anyone got to Floyd about the nice big park he got started up by the high school. He worked on that with a committee of nine for eight years. Floyd got Standard to lease them the parkland for ninety-nine years. Most all the companies in town helped dig the trenches for water pipes, the holes for trees and did the planting.

Dad loved watching his hand picked team play for the fun of the game. After infield practice and lining out the team, he sat on the far end of the bench, kept score, let the players play the game and it worked for him. They played their best to show everybody they were good. And they were.

Basil played center field and he was fast enough to cover some of left and right field. Brother Jesse was the batboy and I played some when we were short on players because of family vacations and stuff. Claude Brown caught our pitchers, Jim Cob and Bob Clark. Hal Haburn played first, Jackie Garner played second, Allen Gilkey was shortstop, Jim Moxley played third. Roy Ethrege, Gene Cottengin, Paul Young, Jerry Taylor played outfield and Ken Aday played outfield and infield...whatever.

Pop's favorite play of the summer was what the Rice's Cubs were all about...fun. Ken Aday got the bunt deal down cold with the lead hand steering the ball to the weakest spot in the infield. Big trouble.

So Ken would surprise bunt a lot and in situations that you absolutely should never bunt. Because he did it so well, he beat out enough bunts to lead the team in batting average.

It was the bottom of the last inning, we were a couple of runs behind, with men on base, two outs and two strikes on old Ken. He lays down this sweet drag bunt and the shit hits the fan.

Ken is off like a shot and everyone is running when the rattled third baseman overthrows first base. When they get to the ball, it is overthrown at third and old Ken came in to score on his own bunt…with men on base…to win the game.

The Cubs loved it while the other team threw a big fit about such a stupid and improper play that should have never been.

Pop filled out the score book, gathered up the gear and left with his winners. They all knew what the game was about… having fun and winning.

A damned fine deal and Pop just smiled.

14. THOSE OFFHAND WALKABOUTS

ONCE IN A while a mood of some kind will strike us and we'll start on a quest of sorts, defined or not. I don't know if we are restless or just curious to see what we might find on our bike-rides or walks. You can walk in some interesting places that a bike couldn't go.

Sometimes our walkabouts are up the big ditch. Me and Troy Hall even do it on stilts, but not too far on those. Troy is the one who's Granddad has an insurance business over on

Skyline by Finster's store. He gives all the kids pencils and rulers with his business and name on them when school starts each year…if you stop by and ask him.

Well, Troy likes those adventures in the ditch and has to laugh at the thought of us on our stilts. Everything is a challenge, jumping, climbing and keeping from falling too much.

Dad made our first good wooden stilts and later, I made several pair. But the simple quick fix was a loop of cord run through holes in cans. You stood on the cans and walked while keeping the tension on the cord to hold the cans to the bottom of your shoes. You could be six or eight inches taller as you walked around with a whole different viewpoint on life. Like standing real high in tall cotton.

People throw odd things in the big ditch and after a heavy rain, the hills and gullies funnel water into the dry gulch and turn it into a wild muddy river at times. Things get stirred up pretty good and it makes for interesting scavenging.

We always hold out hope that we will come around the bend and discover naked girls frolicking about or an old treasure chest or maybe even a sack of money.

On one searching hike down the ditch by myself, without stilts, I saw a couple of whole red bricks in the very bottom of the ditch where it is just a narrow sandy wash path that the lighter rains keep scoured clean. The bricks looked curiously out of place and just too arranged, so I picked them up. And there lay the only hidden treasure I ever found on hundreds of searches of that big ditch.

It must have been a kid who hid it there for some very curious reason. A stash of two one-dollar bills was wrapped around a couple of quarters, a dime and maybe a nickel and a few pennies. I figured it must be stolen if it had to be hidden, so I decided to keep the treasure and the two good bricks. I turned and hurried home a richer man and the pirate could just go to hell...broke.

So far, we are never lucky enough to come around the bend upon naked cavorting girls. But we always hold out hope. Now that I really think about it, we would probably be paralyzed, since naked girls are something you just spy on. I am not having any luck with that either.

When we go up the big ditch, it gradually shrinks into a gully and runs out near the top of the hills. We sometimes turn to go south for a couple of miles, cross big and small gullies and hills, then we follow one down to the Kettleman Plain at the foot of the hills and walk back up to town. As we walk through the sagebrush, we watch for rabbits, lizards, horned toads, snakes, birds and weird bugs like big tarantula spiders.

We hear stories of people surprising sheepherders while they are messing with their sheep but we never have caught anyone yet. We always find bones and check them very carefully in case they might be murder victims dumped for the coyotes to eat. The bones always turn out to be animals, though some of the bigger skeletons look spooky.

The first time we found old Dave's cave-shack and root cellar, back up in one of the bigger gullies, we didn't know what to make of it. Smoke was coming out of a stovepipe that stuck out of the dirt roof covering a shack at the mouth of his cave.

We threw dirt clods at the place to see what would happen and an old man with messed up gray hair and whiskers opened the homemade weathered door and stepped out. In a quiet pleasant voice, he said, "Now boys you really shouldn't be throwing at my house. So...just move along and leave me alone."

I think we were too embarrassed and ashamed to admit it but we knew it was wrong to bother the poor old guy. We taunted him a little more, half-heartedly threw a few more clods and ran over the hill to the next gully and down to the flats and back to town.

When we mentioned the strange event to my folks, They said that the man was a hermit named Dave who had a couple years of college education, a wealthy family some place and for some reason he just wanted to be left alone. We were told to respect his privacy and stay away from there. He later became the caretaker of the Avenal dump and stayed in a larger shack near the dirt road as you entered the dump. It seemed to me that it was not a move up but maybe it was a little more legitimate and a bit safer.

Sometimes we go to treasure hunt the dump. I don't know if Dave ever recognizes us. He probable does but is too much of a gentleman to say anything. We look for discarded wagon wheels and any other things we can use to make go-carts to coast down the hills. I haven't had any success beating the scavengers to the good stuff.

But you might even say Avenal is so small…there is probably only one good wagon in town and it never was thrown away to be scavenged. So there you go.

There are times when I strike out alone on the spur of the moment and do a walkabout out on the flats and swing up into the hills and across to the big ditch and down to the house again. It is peaceful and the hike gets the blood pumping fresh oxygen to my brain, the joints oiled and the adventure energizes me.

My mind wanders through many subjects and travels to all kinds of places, while my body covers considerably less ground. I fanaticize about exotic and exciting adventures on quiet walks that are mostly interrupted by small creature sightings.

I might catch a lizard or a horned toad to play with for a while. I put the reptiles on their back and stroke their sides to put them to sleep or hypnotized them. Then I see how long they will lay on their back before they take off.

A weird rumor about horned toads turned out to be true. Once while I was handling one, I was startled to see blood on my hand where there was no injury. Then I remembered hearing the tale about horny toads squirting blood out of their eyes to startle and escape predators. There was just a trace of blood left near the little guy's eye.

I wonder at the nature in the gullies, hills and plain and enjoy seeing some of the different things that I read about in school. It's a good deal and you don't have to buy a ticket.

15. OUR FUZZY IS NOT A BEAR

A DIFFERENT kind of old guy, who stands out among many nicknamed characters in our town, is a small thin balding man we call Fuzzy. We have lots of nicknames that aren't always favorable…if you know what I mean.

From his comments, Fuzzy gives the impression that he is seldom really focused on matters at hand. Out of step. And as I become old enough to begin observing adults around me, I have discovered that not all grownups are equipped equally.

My guess is that Fuzzy came by his nickname because of

his odd comments that betray, what seems like fuzzy and out of the blue thinking. And, perhaps, his focus isn't helped by a few nips of whatever jug is nearby.

There are times when an event will be under discussion and he will say, "Read it every day in the paper." I wonder if maybe he is just trying to put an issue in it's common perspective. Then he will often add, "Always be yourself and never tell a lie." These three thoughts are repeated so often they lose their impact on us and we consider the source and sometimes discount their value

Fuzzy is at his best in the morning. That's when he does odd jobs in trade for what he needs at the time. Some times it is just a little cash. He can be trusted and is good at many handy tasks.

He is welcome to work in the various gas stations around town. He is good about servicing cars and working hard.

Fuzzy will also sweep and clean bars for spending money, drinks or just to pay his bar tab. Old Jew Margaret, who some say, was the former madam of the Red onion, is owner of the downtown corner Marigold Bar and dance hall. Sometimes Fuzzy helps the old bartender, Pelican Joe, keep the place cleaned up.

I ran out of gas driving Pelican's car and him up to the Springville TB Clinic one time and ruined my reputation as a successful driver. But we did miss the big logging trucks that I was real focused on dodging at the time.

Nick-names can be tough and Pelican Joe does have a real shnozz on him that you couldn't miss.

Our new kid in town, Jimmy Gardener, got ring worms just after he came to town and had to have his head shaved and purple medicine painted on it to get the worms. His head was smooth as a Cue-ball. We laughed and called him Cue-ball and it stuck through grammar and high school.

Of course, Jimmy hated it.

I believe Fuzzy's deal with us is to show up, pitch in and do some chore and earn a dinner invitation, drink or a place to sleep. Sometimes, maybe all of the above.

Our back door opens, then closes…we'd hear footsteps in the kitchen, rattling dishes, then water running in the sink.

Fuzzy was here, hungry and needing an invitation to dinner.

He rolls his own smokes. And as he stands over the sink, with his hands occupied, he tilts his head back and to one side to let the smoke from the cigarette drift up, missing his eyes. The lengthening ash grows in towards his lips with each puff. It gets kind of tense when the ash becomes longer than the cigarette perched in the corner of his mouth.

I don't remember my folks turning him away. He has friends around town and they seem to understand him and make him welcome in their modest houses. I think he can sense when it is time to move on.

It must have been some time during high school that I started to get my head out of my ass and realized I didn't know Fuzzy's regular name. Mom smiled and glanced over at Dad, when I asked and she jokingly said, "Robert Shay… Robert O. Shay."

There is something going on with his name and I sense there would be no serious answer.

He has no real family in Avenal, no official job, no residence and no income taxes. I wondered about his life below the radar screen. Just how did he get into World War II? He served and fought battles in Germany.

We got letters from Fuzzy when he was fighting in the war and killing Germans. He sent us boys three sets of German helmets, ammo belts, bayonets and various other souvenirs. After a while we got tired of them and traded kids for stuff we liked better.

After winning the war, he came back home to Avenal and that was when my first strong memory of him began. Fuzzy seemed like a returning hero in his army uniform. Out of uniform, he became smaller and more common. He would be an occasional guest in our house. Over the years, he has become an honorary Uncle.

Sometimes he borrows a couple of dollars from me. A week or maybe a month or so later he pays me back. Often, I forget about it, but Fuzzy has never failed to pay a debt. His word and name is about all he has and he takes pride in both.

Could be...old Fuzzy is like some preachers who want you to do as they say and not as they do. They just want us to follow the rules to be good people.

And maybe those things he says out of context or out of the blue do make sense, "Always be your self and never tell a lie. Read it everyday in the papers." All three thoughts are good things to remember if you want to stay out of trouble, on the job, with family, friends and avoid brushes with the law. And the good and bad of human nature repeats itself, in news accounts, as history unfolds every day.

These may not be such fuzzy thoughts. Maybe if I keep old Fuzzy's words of wisdom in mind...they may be part of the right deal to have less trouble in life.

Thanks, Fuzzy.

16. SPORTS, LIFE AND ART

I AM TOO small for a junior and still way too slow. Sitting on the damned bench during football and basketball...waiting to get bigger is taking way too long. I did finally make the first string junior varsity baseball team playing first base.

And I am glad to be here. You have to remember how lucky you are when you start to gripe. Car wrecks are usually something you think just happens far away...to people you don't know...and not to a guy like Jimmy.

I remember Jimmy Tinsley most of the way through grammar school. He was big and tough and liked to fight. By the time he was in the eighth-grade, his nose was pulverized into an odd lumpy thing and he had messed up ears. Someone said he and his older brothers fought all the time for the fun of it.

Well, they said one of the older Hunter boys and Jimmy were coming back from a good time over in Huron late one early morning and didn't make a curve coming down off Kettleman Hills on the road in to Avenal.

Someone said Jimmy was hurled through the wooden slats, chicken wire and ragtop of the old car when it rolled. An officer at the scene said Jimmy had wire and wood piercing his chest and was screaming and begging the officer to shoot him. They hauled him off and it took some time for him to finally rest in peace...maybe because he was such a tough fighter.

The Hunter boy survived and we have been driving pretty carefully around here since then and most of us aren't as tough as Jimmy was.

Billy Bob Dealy's sister was also killed in a terrible car accident on her way home from college for a visit. The whole town was stunned because she was so special. Such an unfair thing to happen to her. It just wasn't right, as if God had made an error in judgement or something. Not a good deal.

Getting my name on the wrong list up there with God is a real concern but being a better guy is not easy. I still cuss too much. My buddy, Jim Lawson has convinced me to cut back on my foul mouth and watch my temper. Now that I know what the words actually mean...they don't work very well on my best friends anyway. Giving someone a good cussing doesn't make much sense anymore.

Jim and I are also practicing our running form, hoping that we can improve our speed in sports and make it off the bench.

We get the best crowds for football and basketball Friday night games. Track and baseball are held in the afternoon and most people are working.

During a game the action is always better on the field than on the bench and I hope I grow some to play varsity sports next year. It isn't much fun tackling those big bastards all the time.

Rodney Legate is a hard runner to tackle. Last season, during practice, I caught a knee in the head and had another concussion. But my grades are still staying up to a C average so I am still eligible for sports. I get better grades in art but that doesn't count for too much.

Lloyd is gone again so I'm considered the main artist and the teachers grab me for school projects. I learn new stuff like drawing on glass with colored pencils for slide show programs in the auditorium. I drew all the backgrounds for the junior prom. Other students filled in the colors as I went along so it went fast and was fun. I was proud of the job we did when I saw it all together at the dance.

Sometimes I walk home for lunch with Waymon Davis and Mom always fixes us something to eat. She usually will bake different colored cakes with frosting for an extra treat.

Mom doesn't usually start drinking before lunch. She is fun before she drinks but then she gets to feeling bad and raises hell with Pop, mostly. Its no fun.

Basil gets paid to drive the school bus to Coalinga and goes to college there and is having a good time. He has grown, filled out and is good in basketball and baseball.

He hands me down his jobs as he gets better ones. I have

some spending money now and have two of his weekend yard-jobs. I do the Sisciley's and the Brewster's yards. The money, two or three dollars a week, is a good deal.

Last summer Ollie and Volley Hunter, Neil Myers and a bunch of us hoed tumbleweeds for the State for a dollar and twenty-five cents an hour. It was my first steady summer job. And I always play summer ball in the evenings too.

I taught Dad and myself to take the keys out of the car by getting our old Chrysler New Yorker stolen and trashed. Troy told me to take the keys out of the car but I told him Dad never does. He argued with me and raised hell about how stupid I was as we went in to a school dance. When we came out…he was right and the car was gone. Funny how the kids knew to look in that car for keys in the dark.

I woke Basil and told him about the car. Troy and I had walked all around the school hoping someone had ditched it for a prank but it must have gotten out of hand and gone sour. We woke Pop up and he sat on the edge of the bed, lit a Chesterfield and listened to my story of the car keys. I was petrified at the huge loss to our family and the magnitude of the punishment to come.

Dad rides to work with his crew and they take all take turns driving their cars. Mom has a car about four out of five weeks.

Well, Pop sat there for a while, took a few more puffs and finally said, "I can't say much because I never take the keys out either. Let's go to bed and take care of it later." A couple weeks later it was found and reported trashed and abandoned in the hills.

Dad must have a low regard for investing in more transportation than absolutely needed. Which has resulted in some ugly-assed cars.

I borrow the old Ford Dad bought and it isn't too bad but I like to park it on a hill so I can start it, in case the battery craps out. So I still can go on a date…when I get the nerve to ask a girl out.

We have some real good-looking girls. Growing up with brothers all this time didn't prepare me for girls. They are a real different deal. I don't know exactly what kind of stuff to say to them. A lot of the girls want to go out with upper class-men anyway.

We had an election for officers in Boys Federation and they made me Sergeant at Arms for our senior year. It's the first time I've ever been nominated or elected for anything. I'm supposed to call the meetings to order and keep things under control. We'll have to see about this deal.

17. OCCASIONAL BARBER AND BRAIN SURGEON

POP IS getting out his surgery kit and the young roosters have no idea how miserable they are going to be for the next day or so.

In the shade of our small front porch on the dead end of Yosemite Street and on the wrong side of the big ditch that cuts through Avenal, sometimes Basil and I serve as surgical nurses when Dad operates.

Dad bought this little place so he could sell the place he built down on Whitney Street to the Parkers, who then sold it to Danny Pratt's family. Pop plans to build a new house on the lot we have four blocks south of us near the Uptons.

Over the years Pop has improved his operating skill and speed to a level of excellence. Surgical nurses catch the frisky young roosters and release woozy new capons to mope about for a few hours.

All patients now survive and just occasionally he has a proud or slightly aggressive behaving capon that suggests a slight bit of testicular tissue remains.

It might be a stretch to say he is performing secondary brain surgery but research shows a lot of male plans and actions start with testosterone produced in their male brains, ah…testicles. Regardless, Pop alters attitudes, behaviors, their appearance and certainly tenderizes the roosters with his surgery.

Sometimes a box serves as the operating table and Dad has found that old-fashioned window weights are just about the right amount of restraint needed to hold the wings and legs still during the procedure.

A cord tied to the window weight hangs from one side of the box and is looped around the chicken's legs. On the opposite side of the box, hang the weight from the wings.

The rib area under the wing serves something like an athletic cup to protect the bird's roosterhood…but not from my Dad's scalpel. He makes an inch-long incision between a determined number of ribs behind the wing joint, inserts a retractor to separate the ribs, clamps the exposed testicle, cuts and removes it and the retractor to finish one side. The patient is turned over and the procedure is repeated until we run out of young roosters.

You may wonder how an oil worker in a small town like Avenal could become a very rare and excellent brain surgeon to chickens.

Well, part of it started with a strange incident long ago and seventeen miles up the road from Avenal.

Our Mom was horrified, I was told, when she opened the tiny icebox in our kitchen in Coalinga to find it stuffed full of freshly butchered small chickens.

She had left my Dad to take care of my brother and maybe me, as a baby, (I don't recall hearing the precise timeframe of the event). She had run her Saturday errands and grocery shopped only to return to find her icebox in crisis.

The beginning of the story, I suppose, started when Pop bought a set of hair clippers with scissors and a barber comb to cut my brother Basil Junior's hair and later mine when I came along.

Word travels fast in a small town and Coalinga was no exception. Some of my Dad's friends found a handy resource when cash was short and they wanted a haircut before payday.

One good-timing, fast-living and short sighted fellow got so far behind in haircut favors that he traded Dad the only thing of value he thought he had to spare. And that was a brand new wooden box with a lid that slid out to reveal a booklet of surgery instructions and all the shiny instruments used to caponize chickens for gourmet dining.

Just what an oil worker in a small town needed, right?

Right. Pop's adventurous bent was challenged as he fingered the fine instruments and carefully studied the surgical procedure and thought of plump and tender roasted capons.

During the Great Depression it was not uncommon for families to have a garden for vegetables and a chicken coop for eggs, stewing hens and fryers for meat. We had no space for a cow at our yard, there in town.

When more chicken was needed for the table, we would take a Saturday drive over the hills and across the sagebrush covered alkali flats to Hanford. The large trees and shady lawn of the town-square was an eye-soothing contrast to the landscape we had just crossed.

We would shop for clothes and whatnot, have lunch in Chinatown's Imperial Dynasty and just before leaving town Pop would buy two dozen day-old chicks for a few pennies each and stock up on a fresh supply of chicken feed.

He kept the chicks in a brooder heated with a light bulb till they were ready for the chicken pen and at six weeks he would sort out the roosters for fryers.

This time Dad planned to use his new surgery kit to caponize the young roosters while Mom was away so she wouldn't be upset at the sight of him cutting on the birds.

What he didn't fully anticipate was how live chickens would bleed, squirm and look nothing like a simple diagram in the surgery pamphlet.

There was no quit in Dad resulting in no survivors in the young rooster pen. He believed he could get the procedure down but he just ran out of chickens.

That's how Mom returned to find the icebox serving as morgue for a novice surgeon's piled up practice.

After she settled down, space was cleared for the groceries and some lucky neighbors had tender young chicken for Sunday dinner.

Only after the passage of time, much practice and improving successes did that first horror story in Coalinga become funny. And one of Pop's favorite stories he shared with company.

Of course, over time, word of his surgical skill with chickens also got around Avenal, where we had moved when I was about two years old. Dad would get occasional requests to caponize chickens. And for trade he would sometimes keep a number of capons that was agreed upon in advance.

At some point in time I was delegated to use those old hair clippers to cut my little brother Jesse's hair which took place shirtless and in the back yard on the operating box. He was four years younger and had no say in the matter or any particular interest in hairstyle. No cord or weights were needed to keep him still. Wild horses couldn't drag my older brother Basil to that box for a haircut. Not from his little brother...he was into well-groomed hair.

The spectacle of a kid cutting a littler kid's hair sometimes drew a small crowd of other neighbor youngsters. When they began requesting their turn for haircuts and requests came from a few of the adults like old Fuzzy or Jake, who weren't too particular, I knew my performance had improved enough to trim my own hair on occasion. Now and then Mom has me trim and comb her hair, which is naturally wavy and turning to salt and pepper with age.

Which reminds me...Mom, her brother, Bud, sisters, Anita, Madaline and Norine, all have black wavy hair. Their dad, Grandpa Augere had thicker lips and a broad nose and a darker skin. Mom says her dad was kidded about there being a nigger in the woodpile, back there somewhere.

If fossils tell scientist that Africa is the cradle of mankind, then by God, maybe we are all niggers...just different shades of color, sizes and shapes. We are the same people, but with different languages, names and ideas about the same old God.

I suspect God is bigger than the ones some people fight

over and divide to start new religions…only to preach hate in the name of God against older religions.

Wouldn't the all mighty God want us to just get along?

Anyway, I wish I had black curly hair like Mom. But not the gray, yet. I could handle the nigger in the woodpile crap. I'm handling the Okie bullshit taunting with no trouble. Some people will cuss you and say anything to get your goat.

While I don't mind cutting hair, I suspect I may have to get out of town to avoid my next job promotion to brain surgeon for chickens.

18. LIFE HAS BEEN GOOD

IT IS GOOD to be a big shot Avenal High School senior, I've had some fun along the way but it does mean I will be on my own pretty soon and my life will be what I make of it.

My folks say you can't get anywhere without a college education, so I guess I will have a go at that with my C average.

I have absorbed several concussions in failed train robberies, various sports events, fun gone wrong and survived at least one nervous breakdown getting to this point in my life. I'm not sure where the next surprise will come from, but I will face the future as best I can.

Where will I wind up working in five years and what kind of job will I be doing? And where will my 1953 classmates go when they scatter? Life is full of surprises and the road ahead will surely have some detours.

Pop would have done well in college but at that time, mostly rich kids went to college. After the war a lot of war vets went to college on the GI bill and it started more regular people like us thinking we could go to college.

Basil is doing very well in his second year at Coalinga J.C. and is going up to San Jose St. next year. He is so busy now that he gave me his milk truck-driving job. I get forty-five dollars a month for driving to the Hanford Superior Dairy, to unload empties, load fresh milk and return to Avenal. The owner delivers the milk several hours later and I'm rolling in good money.

Football wasn't much fun at one hundred and thirty-five pounds, being late moving up to the varsity team and over-looked until late in the season. I passed on basketball but did make the varsity baseball team at first base. Corky MacFarlane is the best player we have. I would like to hit the ball like him, but I will leave Avenal High School without any real heroics to talk about. Somewhere, out there, a better deal could be waiting.

Mr. Silva saved me this year from my off beat creativity in English. I am lucky to graduate with my class due to too many hormones, too many Mickey Spilaine sexy detective books and some real immature judgement. All of the gals Mike Hammer runs into…want to get naked and get wild.

Miss. Roberts asked our class to evaluate her performance. With my Mike Hammer hat on, I wrote something to the effect that I would have to do some private in depth study to answer accurately with some certainty on all aspects of her performance.

I was way out of line and offended the young first-year teacher with my outrageous suggestion. Instead of booting me out of school on my butt, Mr. Silva said something to the effect that he would keep an eye on me and if I slipped up again, he would take care of me. I walked the line after that and stayed out of trouble.

If I do make it to college…I will be careful in English classes with any flights of fancy. No more scandals…please.

Dad didn't go to college or have it easy and had his share of surprises along the road that finally led our family to Avenal and our good life here.

All of the adults like Mom and Dad had a life before Avenal and brought different histories to the interesting mix of people living in our young valley town.

In the early 1930s the depression was dragging on, work was scarce and the pay was low most everywhere. Then Dad heard of good money in the valley oil fields. Our family moved to Coalinga where I was born in the summer of 1935.

Like a lot of new arrivals, Dad started as a roughneck on oilrigs and moved up to different jobs as word spread and the openings came. We moved to Avenal sometime in 1937, when I was two. And a couple years later, our little brother Jesse arrived.

Several old sayings we heard around our house as we grew up might give us a clue to our folks surviving the experience of the Great Depression. And their evolved post-depression era philosophy. "Money can't buy happiness." "Live today for tomorrow may never come." "Champagne taste on a beer wage." "There's talkers and then there's doers." "Remember the little boy who cried wolf?"

Dad doesn't worry about the grocery bill at Finster's store or the liquor bill at Rice's. He lets them worry about collecting the money when the tab runs up. He plans adventures for our vacations that are memorable.

Dad reads newspapers, magazines, Jack London, Steinbeck and Hemmingway's new stuff and he likes adventure.

He has worked in the oil fields with different interesting and regular people from all over the south before, during and after the war who could people some of those novels.

In a desolate new oil towns (it takes a while to grow trees in a desert) the popular spots are mostly bars, card rooms and whorehouses. Churches ran the sporting houses out of town. Family guys mostly party at home with drinks from a handy liquor store.

There is some status to be able to drink others under the table. Pop is pretty good at it. The next test is to always show up for work when you have a hangover and never let on that you are suffering. He says you can sweat out a hangover by noon and be OK. I guess you don't have to be an Okie to have Okie pride in being a good worker.

After all Pop had been through during his child hood and the great depression, seeing people with no jobs and starving in the streets of San Francisco, he never complains about work or being tired and he sees that we always have food on the table.

Dad ran compressor plants for Kettleman North Dome Association, worked in repair crews, and headed repair crews. He went to work for Standard Oil Company when they bought-out K.N.D.A. As a crew chief and lead mechanic, he has established record repair times for all categories of big engines and different levels of overhauls. He holds the highest rating of any repairman in the Kettleman Hills oil fields.

Because he refuses to put a worker's job at risk with a poor evaluation, or rat on someone, he is not promoted to the next level on a permanent basis. When he fills in on vacations he gets excellent results supervising the nine repair-crews but he still won't turn in an evaluation on an individual's work.

He can make a lesser mechanic useful by having him scraping or cleaning parts or tools and getting other needed chores done. That frees up the best mechanics to do the tough things. The team effort pays off in consistently better results.

My older brother, Basil Jr., works in the oilfields during the summers during high school and now in college. Dad gives him tips on how to be useful and a good worker but they aren't allowed to work together.

On one occasion, a huge compressor engine had been shut down, repaired, fired back up only to find it had a knock. It was torn down again, fixed, fired up and still was not right. The long delay in production was costing some serious bucks. My brother was in the repair crew and he saw the suits from San Francisco show up and huddle for a consultation.

I guess the order was to get their heads out of their ass and get it fixed…but maybe in San Francisco terms. One of the supervisors left in a company car and returned about a half-hour later with my Dad, an infamous company outlaw.

Basil watched Pop talk to the suits, the supervisor, repair crew and then asked to have the huge compressor engine started.

He walked around the engine with a long handled screwdriver, listening with the handle against his ear. Dad checked all the cylinders, intake and exhaust ports, motioned to shut her down, told them what needed to be done and left in the car. The engine was torn down, the repairs made and the suits left.

That day Basil Jr. saw his Dad as a man among men. A damned good deal for Base.

19. MOM'S DIFFERENT SIDES

MOM HAS had it tough, at times with us three boys, no girls…all of the grubby boy stuff. She must miss the big family gatherings, dressing up and beautiful San Francisco.

Pop brought her down to the rough and hot oil fields during the depression to make good money, feed and shelter his family and be a good husband and father.

The oil money was hard to walk away from after the depression, the war and us being settled in Avenal.

So Mom has tried to hang in there, have some fun and make the best of it like everyone else. She is smart, pretty, slender and has a sense of humor. She learned to cook by helping her father who catered elegant dinners for groups up from The City. They say The City in Novato and all around the bay area.

Her grandpa was a sea captain and a local businessman of some note. Captain Leon Hiribarren was French Basque and went down to sea from a French port when he was a teenager.

Not much is known about why he came to sail into San Francisco and how he gathered his money to start his various businesses. He had a hotel with a restaurant and bar, two cheese factories in Novato and two sailboats for hauling cargo from Petaluma across the bay to San Francisco.

The Captain and his wife had two boys and a girl...Leona, Augere, and Leon Perry Hiribarren. Perry died young and Leona married a man named Crocker over in the bay area and they lost contact with her.

Augere married Anna Casey and he worked for his dad and ran some of the businesses. Then, later, Grandpa Augere had some other jobs. One was a guard at San Quentin for a while. He also worked as a cook on ocean liners out to the Hawiian Islands. So Grandpa could cook. Mom says he would save everything on a pig but the squeal. Headcheese, pickled pigs feet and all that good stuff.

Our company in Avenal is always impressed with Mom's good cooking and the unusual dishes she serves with good humor. And the drinks flow.

Mom is always worried about us kids getting hurt and I guess I just about set the record for scaring the hell out of her and keeping her worried. Mostly I have concussions or bloody cuts from carving wood and one near broken neck And, I guess I went a little crazy for a while one summer.

The movies, radio and reading are the only thing Mom has for entertainment outside of visits with company. The house is pretty quiet with us boys at school and Pop at work. I think she gets the blues sometimes when she's alone.

Then there are bars, not like in San Francisco but they just have to do. Mom and Pop hit the bars now and then and they know everybody in town so it is a party as long as the money lasts.

The drinking can be a bad deal at times. Alcohol and some things just don't mix. You shouldn't drink when you are mad at something or somebody. And never drink when you are depressed. If you are having trouble sober, you'll damned sure have shit-load more when you are a sloppy thinker.

Sloppy thinking comes into the picture at our house when there is too much to drink and old issues are dragged up. Not a good deal.

Dad discuses things with Jake and seems to enjoy the mental challenge of matching facts and wits They never get mad, as far as I know, but Mom does and she can get mean.

That is the sad thing with Mom. I think she remembers the glory days of northern California and then sees her life here and is blue. Add alcohol and she eventually gets on the fight.

When we come home from school and see her eyes are not sharp, we know the shit will hit the fan tonight.

When Pop gets home and sees the situation, he starts some potatoes boiling, opens a can of corn or peas to heat and fries some hamburger or round steak.

We set the table, put on the milk, bread, butter, salt, pepper, worcestershire sauce and wax peppers and sit down at the table.

Sometimes, Mom eats with us and other times, she won't.

When she doesn't eat, Pop tries to tell her she needs food on her empty stomach, but that really sets her off.

Of course I am only guessing, but I think Mom tries to tear Dad down because she feels bad about getting drunk and has to somehow bring Dad to a low level. And I think he knows that.

Working in the oil fields and everywhere else has taught Pop not to let needling, baiting, name-calling get his goat. People can be cruel and will say whatever they think will get under your skin.

So Mom tries to get to Pop by calling him a Nazi son of a bitch, a Gestapo bastard, knowing how much all Americans hated the Germans across the sea. Mom also knew that Pop's grandfather never had a German accent and there were Huffman marriages for generations to non-German girls.

Pop's sister, Evelyn says they are Dutch. I don't know if that is true or that she is just ashamed of her name.

So, the name-calling goes on after we all go to bed, but Mom. She sits in the big chair, talks about carrying all us boys under her heart for nine months and how we don't appreciate it. How she is dying and we will miss her when she is gone. She cusses Pop, who has to get up early and is at work before we get up to go to school.

I have learned to go to sleep after a while. The same record of Mom's favorite insulting material gets played night after night, no surprises. Basil, who has been staying at the Standard bunkhouse during the summers, is now missing the nightly show.

High school is winding down for me but Jesse has four years after me. I hope Mom gets better. She is so good when she is not drinking. I wish Mom could be happy.

20. POP'S ROAD TO AVENAL

MOST OF the people in Avenal, like Pop, have done pretty well with their lives considering the tough circumstances of the times. It could be a rough go.

Dad was born in Healdsburg, California about the time of the big 1907 San Francisco earthquake and the scare sent Grandma back home to tornado country with Dad and Grandpa in tow.

Pop's mother died with the birth of his sister Evelyn. He said he was told the angels came down and took his mother up to heaven. Dad was two years old.

While his father did farm work that was usually sunrise to sunset, my Dad and his sister stayed with grandparents, aunts and uncles, taking turns moving here and there as they grew up. Sometime they were split up to lighten the burden on their relatives.

He must have gotten some special attention as a small child. Dad mentioned to me once that he knew his colors, numbers and letters from wooden blocks before he went to school. He said he also knew what number or letter was on the backside of each colored letter or number of all four sides of the blocks.

During the times he stayed with his sister, she would play the piano and Dad would tap dance in some school programs. I have a picture of Pop just out of High School with a banjo. When he learned to play the twelve-sting banjo, I never heard, though he mentioned that he had played one. I also have a sophisticated pencil drawing of a young girl looking into a bird nest that he made as a teenager.

I remember during the war, watching him draw airplanes that were all shaded with sharp details. Pop was an artist among many other things.

On one ranch of an Aunt and Uncle, they had various livestock, draft horses for heavy fieldwork, saddle horses and horses for their buggy. Pop said one buggy horse was very good if she wasn't hurried. When she trotted, she would loosen up in a mile or so and let fly with gas and manure.

Pop's Aunt and Uncle were running late one Sunday morning. By the time they were dressed for church and the horse and buggy was ready, they were in a stew and took off in a hurry. Dad and his cousins waited and watched the wagon road and sure enough, in a few minutes, here they came back, mad as hell, buggy and fine clothes a stinking mess. They both missed church that Sunday. They had no car but in those days you could have some major horse trouble.

Sometime in there, Dad's grandpa William Huffman was kicked by a horse and died several days later from internal injuries. A number of years later, that memory, combined with my Grandpa's temper and a horse's bad behavior, resulted in a second death. My Grandpa Perry Huffman, who was a hard working and powerfully built man, angrily punched the offending horse in the nose. Even deal. But someone had a dead horse to bury.

Other than that, my grandpa Huffman was usually unruffled under pressure. Like the summer wagon trip Dad and Grandpa took to work a homestead in North Dakota. Some homesteaders told them of break-ins and robberies in the area. The small tarpaper shacks were tolerable in the summer but the harsh winters were too much.

One night a noisy ruckus began in the shack. Grandpa lit the lantern and found a large rattlesnake had gotten his head and part of his body through a knothole in the floor. It was wedged tight and flopping noisily against the wooden boards.

Pop said his Dad picked up a shovel, sliced the first foot or so of snake off clean at the top of the knothole and pitched the wiggling chunk of snake into the yard. He stood the shovel up against the wall, put out the lantern and without a word, went back to bed.

They were in bed one night when they heard horses ride up, foot steps on the porch and a knock at the door. Grandpa reached over, picked up his shotgun, sat up in bed next to

Dad and waited. When someone started breaking in, Grandpa fired a shot through the door, there was a commotion outside and some horses rode away. Grandpa put the shotgun against the wall and settled down to sleep.

Next morning they found blood on the porch and later in a nearby town, they heard about some guy who had passed through town after getting a gunshot wound treated.

My Grandpa Perry came west to California with some of his brothers, mother and mother in law. Dad lived with his father and widowed grandmother in one house on a chicken ranch in Windsor and his sister, Evelyn, lived with their widowed grandmother Cessna in the house next door on their chicken ranch. (Yes, that Cessna, but it was two uncles who built the flying machines.) Times together were good until the ranches were sold and the grandmas moved back to their home places in Iowa and Oklahoma.

Dad stayed in Windsor with his father and finished high school there.

Pop told me of fishing for trout in a small stream just out of town. He would crawl along the wandering creek, peer though the grass, watch the trout check the worm over and take it. He would fish the stream for a couple miles, come out on the road with a nice stringer of trout and hitch a ride back to town. Sometimes a driver would admire his stringer and buy the fish.

There was a lot of baseball played around there at that time and Dad would play as a ringer for some of the small schools. He was sixteen when he graduated from high school so he was able to play several more years. Dad pitched and played first base for some of the local ball clubs. He developed a good fastball with a high hop that was missed or popped up a lot and hard to hit squarely.

Dad played some ball with Uncle Bud Hiribarren, who had some eligible sisters. The one named Vivian became my mom, some years later. Dad's sister and her husband Orval Allen moved out to California.

It turned out that Uncle Orval was a former major league pitcher for a brief time but was banned from organized baseball. I guess the umpire wasn't calling pitches like Orval saw them. The last straw was a call with Orval at the plate with a bat in his hand. The umpire got whacked, Orval was booted and then banned for life from playing professional organized ball.

He still played semi-pro and when he first came out to California, the scouts rushed up to see the new hot pitcher, saw who it was and went back to San Francisco.

One of Dad's best baseball memories was a day when scouts came up from San Francisco to check out Lefty Gomez. Pop was pitching against him and won. Lefty went on to the big leagues. Pop said his size kept him from being a major league prospect. I guess they wanted bigger work-horses. One of his other high points was the time he was scheduled to pitch a homecoming game and they had a banner stretched across the main street that read, "Welcome Home Huffy."

He talked of bumming around the country and riding the rails for six weeks on a dime. His line was that he was hungry and would work for something to eat. Or, he could pay for a dime's worth of food. He said he finally ran into a woman that took the dime.

When times were rough, he and a buddy worked fruit and rode the rails through the valley. He said they developed a fast system for cutting grapes and they would stop early when they had made a good day's pay. By stopping early, they were fresh each day and didn't wear down. The tired workers would pick all day and get a little less done and wear down more each day.

One summer Dad was staying with his uncle Ewel in a farm shack and helped him put up curtains, paint and hang wall paper for the arrival of a mail order bride that was about due to roll in on the train. The next morning, all the wallpaper and fresh paste was gnawed away as far as a rat could reach from the floor.

Uncle Ewel was steamed and that night he waited with lantern lit and horse pistol at hand. When the rat appeared, shots were fired and all hell broke loose. A leg was shot off the pot bellied stove. It fell over and spilled hot coals. The stovepipe collapsed and the shack filled with smoke. They had to scramble to get the coals scooped off the wooden floor and avoid a fire.

A trap was used to kill the rat. Oh, the bride ran off after a few weeks. Pop said she was missing some teeth, was fat, ugly, a mean drunk and not much of a loss.

Dad said a childless couple in the area had a hop ranch, a big brewery and knew his family. They offered to adopt him as a teenager and send him to college and have him run their business. He turned down their offer and stayed with his dad and uncles. He said he had offers later to marry two different wealthy Bay area ladies he'd gotten to know in the City, but passed on being a kept man.

Dad worked several jobs in San Francisco and partied in some of the speakeasies during prohibition. He said he was wearing a brand new three-piece suit and his date and another couple parked their open-top touring sedan on a hill and went into a club. After several drinks, Pop knew something was wrong and got them out of there.

They were crawling and half blind by the time they made

it up the hill to the car. The sun was shining in his eyes the next morning when he woke up. And there were holes eaten in his brand new suit from the thrown up bootleg booze and stomach acid. Those four hung-over drunks must have been a sight you would want to avoid on a sunny Sunday morning. Dad said that was the only new suit he ever wore just once.

Mom and Pop were married in San Francisco. They moved north to Healdsburg and Dad worked on various farms. Dad told me about a dance in the country where the guys would step outside and have a few snorts of bootleg booze during breaks in the music. He got some more bad rot-gut and said he couldn't see. Mom was sober, pregnant and didn't know how to drive the difficult shifting old car. Pop had to drive blind while mom described how he should steer their way home.

Those were the days when good money was just starting to be paid for jobs in the new oilfields down in Californa's central-valley. After Brother Basil was born, Pop made the move south to Coalinga and worked what jobs he could get.

Our oil field days were just beginning.

21. AVENAL'S OFFSPRINGS

I'VE FINISHED High School Mr. Carbiener and you were right about the oil.

The old Kettleman oil field is starting to play out. The newer and deeper field will keep the jobs going a while longer so it will still take a while to go dry. Pop is staying but other workers are transferring to Taft and some are planning on retiring early.

I'm sorry I lost my luck with nominating speeches. My effort for your son Jerry Carbiener fell short and Augie Macias won the student body president race for all the glory next year. But we didn't get in any trouble for decomposing material. And Jerry was too small to kick my butt, plus Augie is a good guy.

We just have a few Mexicans in high school here and they are good students and everybody likes them.

Augie is about the third or fourth Mexican we have elected for student body president in the last few years. Esperonzo Cano was one of the first gals to be elected as an Avenal student body officer.

I haven't worked in the oil fields so I don't get to know many adults in town. Only one kid per family can work summer relief for Standard, but people I don't know come up to me and enjoy talking about my dad.

It's the colorful friends around town and guys in his repair crew Dad talks about like Archie, Toad, Gabby, The Indian, Fuzzy, Blue, Piccolo Pete, Port, Pelican Joe, Smokey, Blackie and Shorty, to name a few. I sense the respect and loyalty he has for them.

Archie Barnett told me about a time Pop was sent home without a day's pay for defying a supervisor. Dad said he realized everyone had worked a bit too long without a break and had gotten overheated. The conditions were unsafe and he ordered them all out for a break. That's when the supervisor drove up and the shit hit the fan.

Archie said, "That wasn't right. We should have all walked out with Huffy." His eyes got misty and he was agitated again, just thinking about it.

Archie and all of Pop's first crew have become lead mechanics with their own crews and use Dad's team style of working.

I have my high school diploma but work is scarce. I have worked one week on the Avenal garbage truck for the helper who was on vacation. Then I worked two weeks for R.T. Dealy Construction Co. digging ditch and shoveling sand and gravel into a cement mixer. That is it for the long, hot, slow summer…three weeks of work.

Some were old guys working and sweating along side of me and it hit me that we were all making the same money. And I could be doing work like this until I'm an old man…like them…not a very good deal.

School is about to start at Visalia College of Sequoias where my high school art teacher, Mr. Russell now teaches college art classes.

There is about one hundred and seventy-five dollars I have in the bank, saved from the three weeks of summer work. Money that will help get me going for a couple of months while I find some part time work. If not, I will dropout, join the army and make another run at college later. Life is good and maybe it will get better.

There always seems to be some evil bastards out there who want to take over the world. Grandpa Perry told me when we were fighting the Nazis and the Japs that we couldn't trust Russia. I argued that they were our friends and were helping fight Hitler. Well, Grandpa was right.

We whipped Germany and Japan then made them give back all the countries they took and helped our enemies re-build. Russia took part of Germany and all the little countries it could get their hands on and now they have an A-bomb. Some people are thinking about building bomb shelters.

Some say the pessimists are learning Chinese rather than Russian. They are all communists and are moving in on the weak countries around the world. Some of my buddies have joined the service and are heading to Korea. I am registered for the draft and when they come after me…I will go.

Until then I will do the best I can to have a good life.

While I am moving on, over the Kettleman Hills into the rest of the world, I will hold on to these memories. There will be times that I will remember Avenal when I'm in some far away place, with time to reflect…and that will be good.

Dad said something simple, yet clear and true to Basil when he was having trouble with money in college. I hear those words when things get tough, "Finish what you start… anyone can quit."

I'll try to finish college, Pop.

22. AVENAL'S HISTORIC BIRTH

Sources: Kettleman Hills by James W. Beebe,
Personal observations and conversations,
The Avenal Historical Society scrap books.

Labor Pains

March 21, 1927 - Milham Elliot well No.1 is started and it is drilled much deeper than all earlier wells…where Yocut Indians once hunted and gathered food.

October 5, 1927 - Milham Elliot well No.1 strikes a monster oil field in Kettleman Hills and blows out of control at 5,000 feet.

It is almost pure gasoline and very dangerous.

November of 1928 - After a number of difficulties and great loss of oil and gas, the gigantic Milham Elliot well No. 1 is brought under control.

The greatest oil boom in the San Joaquin Valley sets off a

huge spending spree on new deeper wells.

Kings County resources doubles in value and tax rates for county taxpayers decline because of the huge amounts of oil company taxes.

Up to this time, various wildcat wells were being drilled in the Kettleman Hills, all with no commercial production value. Men drove from Coalinga and various towns to work the oil fields.

With the big Milham Elliot strike, more deep wells are drilled, roads are built to carry heavy equipment and pipelines are being laid for water, gas and oil. Standard and Milham camps are providing living quarters.

Birth

February of 1929 - The first small building to go up, on what will soon be Avenal, is built by the welder, Allan Arther and named Paco Welding Shop. The new boomtown begins as mostly a tent city on leased land.

April of 1929 - Avenal is laid out and building sites are available to lease from Standard oil. $5.00 per month for houses and $15 to $30 for businesses.

Soon MacFarlane and Schmidt build and run a restaurant and barbershop.

Business in the first two houses of ill repute, The White Swan and the Blue Goose is serviced in tents. The Red Onion is the last to come and go and it is located in a house south of town.

Place names in the area such as Avenal Ranch, Avenal Gap, Avenal School in Sunflower Valley, Avenal Canyon,

Avenal Creek and various landmarks called Avenal existed before the new town. Avenal derives from avena, Spanish for oats or oat field.

May of 1929 - Various large supply houses move to Avenal such as Cross Lumberyard and hardware store and Republic Supply Co. Warehouse.

Barney Leckenby moved in the first house. Others are being moved from nearby communities. New construction is underway.

August of 1929 – The first natural gas from Kettleman Hills Reaches San Francisco and more pipelines are being laid.

Standard Oil Co. Hospital is under construction and the electric system for the town is under way.

October of 1929 - Avenal has a school building being prepared for attendance of twenty-five children. Standard Oil Co. moved it in from the Coalinga area.

November of 1929 - Avenal has 16 families and 15 business establishments.

December of 1929 - The Post Office is established in Avenal and there are 22 active oil rigs in Kettleman Hills.

1930 – Avenal has water and gas available and the oil field now has 5 absorption plants in operation.

Marie Eads is appointed Post Master in August.

Ed Burch is the first constable.

1931 – First telephone service is available and a branch library is maintained in Avenal which has about 250 families and a population of 1,500.

In a concerted move to cut massive gas waste, Shell Oil

and Standard Oil partner with PG&E to lay pipelines to send the excess natural gas to serve coastal and bay area markets.

1932 – Reef School District of Avenal and Sunset of Kettleman City join.

1933 – Avenal Airport is leveled and oiled.

Avenal's first weekly newspaper is The Avenal Rotary and is published by Dillingham and Woodson.

Avenal organizes its first Woman's Club.

1935 – Avenal Elementary school brick building is finished

Avenal Theater opens October 19. Up to this date, shows were watched in a tent on wooden benches. Standard Oil Co. built the theater.

(This author is born in Coalinga)

1936 – Production reaches it's peak of 38 million barrels in Kettleman oil fields.

Avenal gets a new Post Office, Bank of America and Library built by Standard Oil Co.

1937 – Avenal students get a new High School built with Kings County oil taxes.

(My family moves to Avenal)

1938 – The first Avenal High School Class Laneva is printed.

1942 – Japanese bomb Pearl Harbor and we are at war with Japan and Germany.

1945 – We win World War II.

1946 – Avenal Park is built by local companies on land leased from Standard Oil for 99 years. Floyd Rice and his committee of nine worked for eight years to get the deal done.

1947 – The Avenal Grammer School is expanded.

1951 – Avenal Hospital is dedicated September 7, 1951

1952 – The Kettleman Hills oilfield production is getting near the bottom of the barrel.

1953 – Avenal High School gets a new auditorium and class rooms.

(And I graduate and move to Visaila to attend college)

Perry, Jesse and Basil Huffman

The Huffman boys, Easter Sunday, 1940, pose holding tinfoil covered candy on Whitney Street, next to the big ditch.

Across the ditch, you can see an outhouse, piled material and an old truck in the back yard of our neighbor, Piccolo Pete, who was a lawyer.

Perry is about five years old, Jesse is about one and Basil is about seven years of age.

At this time Dad was building a garage in the back yard. He would sell our trailer, demolish the room next to it and the big covered shelter. Then, he would build our new house with a big basement.

Old Time Avenal

The Huffmans came down town for the show, the library
and to shop.

The Huffman Riverside Villa

The two older Huffman boys, with our trick dog Sport, in
front of our first Huffman place in Avenal. You can just make
out, through the latticework, our trailer, which served as our
bedroom and opened into the wooden room on the right.

It contained a wood stove, kitchen and kitchen table
and chairs.It was our all-purpose room with a fine view
overlooking the ditch. The sheltered area to the left was a
carport and breezeway

106

Jesse Huffman

Jesse was our building site and parking lot security guard.

Dad was building our new house to replace the trailer villa shown in the picture just above. This is sometime around 1942.

Vivian and Basil Huffman
Mom and Dad Huffman visiting Mom's childhood home in
Novato California on September 11, 1955.

Hats, cane and parasol were borrowed from old family trunk
for this fun picture.

Common Oil Field Terms

Work times;

Morning tower – first eight hour shift

Afternoon tower –second eight hour shift

Evening tower – third eight-hour shift

Compressor plants – compress gas into liquid

Cooling towers – cool the gas and oil

Core – sample of drilling material

Derrick – oil drilling rig

Drill Bit – cuts through formations on the tip of drill pipe

Drip – condensation that is unleaded gasoline

used by workers during the war when gas was rationed

Driller – boss on an oil rig

Duster – dry well hole…no oil

Fishing – recovering broken drill equipment from the hole

Gusher – oil strike that flows or gushes under pressure

Mud – A mixture that is pumped down the wells to control
the well pressure

Pipeliners – lay pipelines

Plant Operators – oil engines, operate plant and keep track
of production

Repairman – repair compressor engines and anything else

Rigs – oil derricks

Rigging – well setup

Riggers – build oil derricks

Rough necks – handle drill pipe

Roustabouts – general-all-around go-for and do-stuff guys

Stand of drill pipe – length of drill pipe

Sump - basin to catch and hold excess oil

Tool pushers – oversee drilling crews and answer to engineers

Welders – repairs equipment

Wildcat drillers - independent operators

ISBN 141205891-0